AF447585

The Emotion Code: Decoding Emotional Intelligence

Adam Poliman

Published by Adam Poliman, 2023.

While every precaution has been taken in the preparation of this book, the publisher assumes no responsibility for errors or omissions, or for damages resulting from the use of the information contained herein.

THE EMOTION CODE: DECODING EMOTIONAL INTELLIGENCE

First edition. August 24, 2023.

Copyright © 2023 Adam Poliman.

ISBN: 979-8223735625

Written by Adam Poliman.

Also by Adam Poliman

The Power of Time: Transform Your Life through Effective Time Management

Unleashing The Power Of Reading

Unlocking the Power of Critical Thinking: Strategies for Effective Problem-Solving

Efficiency Unleashed: Mastering Productivity Tips and Hacks for Success

The Art of Social Intelligence: Mastering the Skills of Effective Communication

Destined For Greatness: Mastering The Art Of Goal Setting

Mind Over Temptation: Building Self-Discipline In A Distracted World

The Emotion Code: Decoding Emotional Intelligence

The Growth Mindset Advantage: Thriving Through Lifelong Learning

Unleashing Your Potential: A Guide To Personal Development And Self-Improvement

Watch for more at https://optimizationtime.com.

Do you ever feel like emotions are a puzzle, a complex web of thoughts and feelings that you can't quite decipher? Like trying to unravel a knot that seems impossibly tangled?

Well, imagine if there was a key, a code that could help you decode and understand your emotions with clarity and precision. That's exactly what 'The Emotion Code: Decoding Emotional Intelligence' aims to do.

In this book, we will delve into the fascinating world of emotional intelligence, a concept that has gained significant attention in recent years. Think of emotional intelligence as a compass, guiding you through the intricacies of your emotions, helping you navigate through life's challenges with greater self-awareness and empathy.

Through exploring the different facets of emotional intelligence, such as emotional self-awareness, self-regulation, motivation, and empathy, we will uncover the profound impact that emotional intelligence can have on our personal and professional relationships.

So, get ready to embark on a journey of self-discovery and growth as we unlock the code to emotional intelligence.

I. Introduction to Emotional Intelligence

Understanding Emotional Intelligence is crucial in developing self-awareness and empathy towards others.

The Five Pillars of Emotional Intelligence, which include self-awareness, self-regulation, motivation, empathy, and social skills, provide a framework for cultivating emotional intelligence.

Recognizing the impact of emotional intelligence on mental health allows individuals to better navigate and manage their emotions, leading to improved well-being.

Additionally, Emotional Quotient Testing offers a valuable tool for assessing and understanding one's emotional intelligence, enabling personal growth and increased interpersonal effectiveness.

Understanding Emotional Intelligence

Let's delve into the fascinating world of Emotional Intelligence (EQ).

EQ is the ability to recognize, understand, and manage your own emotions, as well as the emotions of others.

It is different from IQ, which measures cognitive intelligence, as EQ focuses on social and emotional skills.

Developing and honing your EQ is crucial, as it plays a significant role in personal and professional success.

The history of Emotional Intelligence dates back to the early 20th century, with the work of psychologists such as Edward Thorndike and Howard Gardner, who laid the foundation for this concept.

What is Emotional Intelligence?

To truly grasp emotional intelligence, you must delve into the intricacies of what it means to be emotionally intelligent.

Emotional intelligence is the ability to identify, understand, and manage your own emotions, as well as recognize and empathize with the emotions of others. It involves being aware of your own feelings and how they impact your thoughts and actions.

It also means being able to navigate and handle relationships effectively, by understanding and responding to the emotions of those around you. Emotional intelligence is not just about being able to control your emotions, but also about having the capacity to perceive and interpret the emotions of others accurately.

It requires a level of self-awareness, self-regulation, social awareness, and relationship management. Developing emotional intelligence can lead to improved communication, stronger relationships, and better overall well-being. It's an essential skill that allows you to navigate the complexities of human interactions with empathy, understanding, and resilience.

Difference between IQ and EQ

The disparity between IQ and EQ can be likened to the contrast between a computer's processing power and a human's ability to connect on an emotional level.

While IQ measures intellectual abilities such as logical reasoning and problem-solving skills, EQ focuses on emotional intelligence, which encompasses self-awareness, empathy, and social skills.

Although both are important, EQ plays a crucial role in building and maintaining relationships, understanding others' perspectives, and managing emotions effectively.

Unlike IQ, which is relatively fixed, EQ can be developed and improved over time through self-reflection, empathy training, and practicing emotional regulation.

Enhancing your emotional intelligence can lead to better communication, increased empathy, and a deeper understanding of yourself and others.

By recognizing and valuing the importance of emotional intelligence, you can unlock a whole new level of connection and interpersonal effectiveness.

Importance of Emotional Intelligence

Developing and honing your ability to understand and connect with others on a deeper level can greatly enhance your relationships and overall effectiveness in navigating social interactions.

Emotional intelligence plays a crucial role in our personal and professional lives. It allows us to accurately perceive and manage our own emotions while also understanding and empathizing with the emotions of others.

By cultivating emotional intelligence, you can improve your communication skills, build stronger interpersonal connections, and effectively resolve conflicts. It enables you to navigate complex social situations with ease, adapt to different personalities, and respond to challenges with empathy and understanding.

Moreover, emotional intelligence helps in building resilience, managing stress, and promoting mental well-being. By recognizing and regulating emotions, you can make more informed decisions, collaborate effectively, and lead with empathy.

In a world that is increasingly interconnected, having a high level of emotional intelligence is not just a valuable asset but an essential skill for personal and professional success.

History of Emotional Intelligence

Picture this: it's the 18th century, and you're at a royal ball, where the art of understanding and connecting with others on a deeper level is just as important as the grandeur of the occasion.

Emotional intelligence may not have been a term coined back then, but its roots can be traced back to this era. It was during this time that philosophers and thinkers began to recognize the significance of emotions in human interactions. They understood that emotions played a pivotal role in shaping relationships and influencing behavior.

Fast forward to the 20th century, and scholars like Daniel Goleman and Peter Salovey brought emotional intelligence into the mainstream. They emphasized the importance of understanding and managing emotions, not just in interpersonal relationships but also in personal well-being and success.

Today, emotional intelligence is recognized as a vital skill in navigating the complexities of human interactions and achieving personal growth. It allows us to recognize and empathize with others' emotions, communicate effectively, and make informed decisions.

So, as you attend that royal ball in your mind, remember the history of emotional intelligence and the profound impact it has had on our understanding of human emotions and connections.

The Five Pillars of Emotional Intelligence

In this discussion, we'll explore the five pillars of emotional intelligence:

1. Self-awareness: You can become more self-aware by focusing on these pillars.

2. Self-regulation: You can better regulate your emotions by understanding and developing your own emotional intelligence.

3. Motivation: By finding motivation from within, you can enhance your emotional intelligence.

4. Empathy: Understanding and empathizing with others is crucial in developing emotional intelligence.

5. Social skills: Enhancing your social interactions is another key aspect of emotional intelligence.

Self-awareness

Self-awareness is a fascinating aspect of emotional intelligence that allows you to truly understand and appreciate yourself. It's the ability to recognize your own emotions, thoughts, and behaviors, and how they impact those around you.

By developing self-awareness, you gain a deeper understanding of your strengths and weaknesses, your values and beliefs, and your triggers and patterns. This insight enables you to make more conscious choices and take control of your emotions, rather than being controlled by them.

Self-awareness also allows you to have a greater sense of empathy and understanding towards others, as you become more attuned to their emotions and experiences. It's a journey of self-exploration and self-acceptance that leads to personal growth and fulfillment.

So take the time to reflect on yourself, your emotions, and your actions. Explore who you are at your core, and embrace both the light and the shadows within you. Your journey of self-awareness won't only enhance your emotional intelligence but also empower you to live a more authentic and meaningful life.

Self-regulation

Imagine yourself as a skilled sailor navigating the turbulent seas of your own emotions, using self-regulation as your compass to steer towards calm waters and find balance in the storm.

Self-regulation is the art of managing and controlling one's emotions, thoughts, and behaviors in a way that promotes well-being and positive outcomes. It requires a deep understanding of oneself, the ability to recognize and acknowledge emotions as they arise, and the capacity to respond to them in a healthy and constructive manner.

Through self-regulation, you can cultivate emotional intelligence, which is the key to developing resilience, building meaningful relationships, and achieving personal growth. By practicing self-regulation, you can avoid impulsive reactions, make sound decisions, and effectively cope with stress and adversity. It allows you to pause, reflect, and choose your response rather than being driven solely by instinct or external circumstances.

Self-regulation empowers you to harness the power of emotions, using them as valuable sources of information and motivation rather than being controlled by them. It enables you to navigate the ups and downs of life with grace and composure, fostering a sense of inner peace and fulfillment.

So, imagine yourself as that skilled sailor, using self-regulation to navigate the vast ocean of emotions, finding serenity amidst the storm and embracing the transformative power of emotional intelligence.

Motivation

Motivation plays a crucial role in guiding you towards your goals and driving you to take action in pursuit of your desires. It is the fuel that ignites your passion and propels you forward, even in the face of obstacles and setbacks.

Without motivation, it can be easy to get stuck in a rut and lose sight of what truly matters to you. When you're motivated, you're more likely to persevere through challenges, stay focused on your objectives, and maintain a positive mindset.

Motivation is not only about setting ambitious goals, but also about finding the inner drive and determination to turn those goals into reality. It's about understanding what truly inspires and excites you, and using that knowledge to fuel your actions.

By harnessing your motivation, you can tap into your full potential and achieve remarkable success. So, take a moment to reflect on what truly motivates you and let that be the driving force behind your actions.

Empathy

Understanding the feelings and experiences of others, and being able to connect with them on a deeper level, is a key aspect of being in touch with our own humanity. Empathy allows us to step into someone else's shoes and truly understand their perspective, emotions, and struggles.

It is the ability to recognize and acknowledge the pain or joy that others are going through, and to respond with compassion and understanding. When we practice empathy, we are able to build stronger relationships, foster trust, and create a safe space for others to express themselves. By listening attentively, validating their emotions, and offering support, we can help alleviate their suffering and make a positive impact in their lives.

Empathy is not just about feeling sorry for someone or offering sympathy, but rather about genuinely understanding and connecting with others on a profound level. It is about recognizing that we're all human beings with our own unique experiences, and that we all deserve to be seen, heard, and understood.

Through empathy, we can bridge the gap between ourselves and others, and cultivate a sense of unity and compassion in our communities and beyond.

Social skills

Now that you've delved into the importance of empathy, it's time to explore another crucial aspect of emotional intelligence: social skills.

Developing strong social skills allows you to navigate various social situations with ease and effectiveness. It involves a combination of verbal and non-verbal communication, active listening, and the ability to understand and manage your own emotions in a social context.

Social skills enable you to build and maintain meaningful relationships, collaborate effectively, and positively influence others. They empower you to connect with people on a deeper level, fostering trust, respect, and understanding.

By honing your social skills, you can navigate the complexities of social interactions with grace and finesse, ultimately leading to more fulfilling and successful relationships.

Emotional Intelligence and Mental Health

Emotional Intelligence plays a crucial role in managing stress, anxiety, and overall mental health.

By developing your EQ, you can better understand and regulate your emotions, which in turn can help reduce stress and anxiety levels.

Additionally, having a high EQ can contribute to a lower risk of depression, as it allows you to effectively navigate challenging emotions and build resilience.

EQ's impact on Stress

By harnessing the power of emotional intelligence, you can effectively manage your stress levels and cultivate a more balanced and fulfilling life.

When you have a high level of emotional intelligence, you're able to recognize and understand your emotions, as well as the emotions of others. This self-awareness allows you to identify when stress is building up and take proactive steps to manage it.

You can develop coping mechanisms and techniques that work specifically for you, such as deep breathing exercises, mindfulness practices, or engaging in activities that bring you joy and relaxation.

Additionally, emotional intelligence helps you to build strong relationships and communicate effectively, which can reduce stress in your personal and professional life. When you have healthy and supportive connections, you have a network of people who can provide emotional support and help you navigate challenging situations.

Overall, by honing your emotional intelligence, you have the tools to effectively manage stress and create a more harmonious and fulfilling life.

Anxiety and Emotional Intelligence

When you tap into your emotional intelligence, you become adept at recognizing and managing anxiety, creating a sense of calm and clarity in your life.

Anxiety can be overwhelming and debilitating, but by developing your emotional intelligence, you gain the tools to navigate through these challenging emotions.

By understanding the root causes of your anxiety and identifying the triggers that set it off, you can begin to address and resolve them.

Emotional intelligence allows you to recognize when your anxiety is disproportionate to the situation at hand and helps you respond in a more balanced and rational manner. It enables you to regulate your emotions, preventing them from spiraling out of control and causing unnecessary stress.

Moreover, emotional intelligence fosters empathy and self-awareness, allowing you to understand and express your feelings effectively.

This self-awareness empowers you to communicate your needs and boundaries, reducing anxiety-inducing conflicts and promoting healthier relationships.

By harnessing your emotional intelligence, you can transform anxiety into an opportunity for growth and self-discovery, ultimately leading to a more fulfilling and balanced life.

EQ and Depression

Developing your EQ can be a powerful tool in managing and overcoming depression. Studies have shown that individuals with higher emotional intelligence are significantly less likely to experience depressive symptoms. By understanding and managing your emotions effectively, you can better navigate the challenges and setbacks that often contribute to feelings of depression.

Emotional intelligence allows you to recognize and regulate your emotions, as well as understand the emotions of others. This self-awareness and empathy help you build stronger relationships and support systems, which are crucial in maintaining mental well-being.

Additionally, individuals with high EQ are better equipped to cope with stress, adapt to change, and problem-solve effectively, all of which are important skills in managing depression. By developing your emotional intelligence, you can gain a deeper understanding of yourself and others, leading to improved mental health and overall well-being.

Emotional Quotient Testing

When it comes to understanding and developing your emotional intelligence, EQ testing plays a crucial role. These tests are designed to measure your emotional quotient and provide insights into how well you understand and manage your own emotions, as well as how effectively you navigate social interactions.

There are various types of Emotional Intelligence tests available, each focusing on different aspects such as self-awareness, empathy, and relationship management.

Interpreting your EQ test results can be a valuable tool in identifying areas of strength and areas that may need improvement, allowing you to further enhance your emotional intelligence skills and overall well-being.

Importance of EQ testing

Discover the incredible power of EQ testing and unlock your true emotional potential.

By assessing your emotional intelligence through EQ testing, you gain valuable insights into your ability to understand and manage your emotions effectively.

This testing allows you to identify areas of strength and weakness, providing you with the opportunity to develop and improve your emotional intelligence skills.

EQ testing not only helps you to understand yourself better but also enhances your ability to navigate social interactions and build strong relationships.

It allows you to recognize and regulate your emotions, enabling you to respond to challenging situations with resilience and adaptability.

Through EQ testing, you can cultivate self-awareness, empathy, and effective communication skills, ultimately leading to personal growth and success in various aspects of your life.

So, take the first step in unlocking your true emotional potential by embracing the importance of EQ testing.

Different types of Emotional Intelligence tests

Now that you understand the significance of testing emotional intelligence (EQ), let's dive into the various types of tests available to decode this crucial aspect of human nature.

Testing EQ is not a one-size-fits-all approach, as there are different methods to assess emotional intelligence. These tests range from self-report questionnaires to performance-based assessments, each designed to uncover different aspects of emotional intelligence.

By exploring these different types of tests, you can gain a deeper understanding of your own emotional intelligence and how it affects your interactions with others.

So, let's embark on this journey of self-discovery and unravel the mysteries of emotional intelligence together.

How to interpret EQ test results

To truly understand your EQ test results, you may initially feel overwhelmed by the data and wonder how it applies to your everyday life. However, by taking the time to analyze and reflect on your results, you can uncover valuable insights about your interpersonal skills and ultimately enhance your relationships with others.

Remember, emotional intelligence is not a fixed trait but rather a skill that can be developed and improved upon. Your test results serve as a starting point for self-awareness and growth. Look for patterns and themes in your scores, and consider how they align with your experiences and interactions with others.

Are there areas where you excel and areas where you struggle? Pay attention to any areas where you may have a high level of emotional intelligence as well as areas that may need improvement. Use this information to guide your personal development journey and seek out resources or strategies that can help you strengthen your weaker areas.

By interpreting your EQ test results in this way, you can gain a deeper understanding of yourself and your emotions, leading to more fulfilling and meaningful relationships with others.

II. Emotional Self-Awareness

In this discussion, we'll explore the subtopic of emotional self-awareness. We'll focus on its definition and importance, developing this skill, and its impact on relationships. Understanding and recognizing your own emotions is essential for personal growth and effective communication. By developing emotional self-awareness, you can better understand your own needs and desires, leading to improved self-confidence and decision-making.

Additionally, this increased self-awareness can positively impact your relationships, as it allows for more authentic and empathetic connections with others.

Definition and Importance

When it comes to emotional self-awareness, it refers to your ability to recognize and understand your own emotions. This skill is crucial because it allows you to accurately identify how you feel and why, which can help you effectively navigate through challenging situations.

In fact, research has shown that individuals with high emotional self-awareness tend to have better mental health, stronger relationships, and higher levels of overall well-being. So, developing this skill can greatly contribute to your personal and professional success.

Defining Emotional Self-awareness

Emotional self-awareness allows you to truly understand and connect with your innermost feelings, leading to a profound sense of self-discovery and growth.

It is the ability to recognize and acknowledge your emotions in the present moment, without judgment or suppression.

By developing emotional self-awareness, you become more attuned to your own needs, desires, and motivations, which enables you to make better decisions and navigate through life with greater clarity and authenticity.

This self-awareness also enhances your understanding of how your emotions impact your thoughts, behaviors, and relationships, allowing you to cultivate healthier and more meaningful connections with others.

It is through this process of self-reflection and introspection that you can uncover deep-seated patterns and beliefs that may be holding you back, and begin to heal and transform them.

Emotional self-awareness is not about being overly self-absorbed or indulging in self-pity, but rather about developing a compassionate and non-judgmental relationship with yourself.

It is a journey of self-discovery and growth that requires patience, curiosity, and a willingness to explore the depths of your own emotional landscape.

Benefits of emotional self-awareness

One of the key benefits of emotional self-awareness is that it acts as a compass, guiding you through the unpredictable storms of life and helping you navigate towards calmer waters.

When you're aware of your emotions, you can better understand why you feel the way you do and how it affects your thoughts and actions. This self-awareness allows you to make more informed decisions and respond to challenging situations in a more balanced and constructive manner.

By recognizing your emotions, you can also effectively communicate your needs and boundaries to others, fostering healthier relationships and reducing conflicts.

Moreover, emotional self-awareness enables you to identify and address any underlying issues or patterns that may be holding you back from reaching your full potential. It empowers you to take control of your emotional well-being and actively work towards personal growth and fulfillment.

Ultimately, by cultivating emotional self-awareness, you can enhance your overall emotional intelligence and lead a more meaningful and satisfying life.

Link between self-awareness and success

Achieving success depends on self-awareness, as it allows you to navigate through life's challenges and make informed decisions, leading to a more fulfilling and meaningful journey.

When you're self-aware, you have a deep understanding of your emotions, strengths, weaknesses, and values. This knowledge enables you to identify your goals and align them with your authentic self.

By being aware of your emotions, you can effectively manage them and respond to situations in a balanced and rational manner. This emotional intelligence gives you an advantage in both personal and professional relationships, as you're better equipped to understand and empathize with others.

Self-awareness also helps you recognize and learn from your mistakes, leading to personal growth and development. Ultimately, it's through self-awareness that you can unlock your full potential and achieve success in all areas of your life.

Developing Emotional Self-Awareness

To improve your emotional self-awareness, there are a few key steps you can take.

First, practice mindfulness by paying attention to your thoughts, feelings, and bodily sensations in the present moment without judgment. This can help you become more attuned to your emotions and understand their triggers.

Additionally, self-reflection is crucial in developing emotional self-awareness as it allows you to examine your thoughts, actions, and reactions to better understand yourself and how you relate to others.

By incorporating these practices into your daily life, you can deepen your understanding of your emotions and enhance your emotional intelligence.

Steps to improve emotional self-awareness

Improving emotional self-awareness starts with recognizing and understanding your own emotions.

Take the time to pause and reflect on how you're feeling in different situations. Pay attention to the physical sensations in your body and the thoughts that arise. This self-reflection will help you gain insight into your emotional patterns and triggers.

Additionally, practicing mindfulness can enhance your emotional self-awareness. By bringing your attention to the present moment, you can observe your emotions without judgment. Notice how they come and go, and how they affect your thoughts and actions.

It's also important to seek feedback from others. Ask trusted friends or family members for their perspectives on how you handle emotions. This external input can provide valuable insights and help you see blind spots in your self-awareness.

Finally, journaling can be a powerful tool for improving emotional self-awareness. Write down your thoughts and feelings on a regular basis. This process of putting your emotions into words can help you gain clarity and understanding.

By actively working on improving your emotional self-awareness, you can develop a greater understanding of yourself and better navigate your emotions.

Practice Mindfulness

Practicing mindfulness is like tending to the garden of your mind, allowing you to cultivate a deeper understanding of your inner landscape.

By engaging in the present moment and paying attention to your thoughts, feelings, and sensations without judgment, you can develop a greater sense of self-awareness.

Mindfulness helps you become more attuned to your emotions, enabling you to recognize and acknowledge them as they arise. This heightened awareness allows you to respond to your emotions in a more deliberate and constructive manner, rather than reacting impulsively.

It also helps you identify patterns and triggers that may be contributing to certain emotional states, giving you the opportunity to address and resolve them.

As you practice mindfulness regularly, you will develop a stronger connection to your emotions, leading to increased emotional intelligence and overall well-being.

So, take a moment each day to be fully present and observe the thoughts and emotions that pass through your mind. Embrace them with curiosity and compassion, and watch as your emotional self-awareness blossoms.

Importance of Self-reflection

Take a moment to pause and truly reflect on yourself, for self-reflection holds the key to unlocking a deeper understanding and connection with your innermost thoughts and emotions.

By taking the time to reflect on your experiences, actions, and reactions, you gain valuable insights into your own patterns, motivations, and beliefs.

Self-reflection allows you to explore the reasons behind your emotions and behaviors, helping you to identify any negative patterns or limiting beliefs that may be holding you back.

It also provides an opportunity for growth and personal development, as you can learn from past experiences and make conscious choices that align with your values and goals.

Through self-reflection, you can cultivate a greater sense of self-awareness and emotional intelligence, enabling you to navigate relationships and challenges with more clarity and empathy.

So, take a moment to pause, breathe, and reflect on yourself, for it is through this practice that you can truly uncover the depths of your emotional intelligence and unlock your fullest potential.

Emotional Self-Awareness and Relationships

In personal relationships, emotional self-awareness plays a crucial role in fostering healthy connections. Being aware of your own emotions allows you to communicate effectively and understand the emotions of others, leading to better understanding and empathy.

In the workplace, self-awareness is equally important as it helps you navigate conflicts, manage stress, and build strong relationships with colleagues.

Additionally, emotional self-awareness is a key trait in effective leadership, as it allows leaders to understand and manage their own emotions, as well as the emotions of their team members, leading to improved collaboration and overall success.

How emotional self-awareness affects personal relationships

Understanding your own emotions plays a crucial role in the dynamics of your personal relationships. When you have emotional self-awareness, you're better able to identify and understand your own feelings. This allows you to communicate them effectively to your partner or loved ones.

This not only helps you express your needs and desires, but it also fosters empathy and understanding in your relationships. By being aware of your own emotions, you can also better manage them and prevent them from negatively impacting your interactions with others.

Additionally, emotional self-awareness allows you to recognize patterns and triggers in your emotions. This helps you navigate conflicts and challenges in a more constructive and compassionate way.

Overall, developing emotional self-awareness is essential for building and maintaining healthy and fulfilling personal relationships.

Self-awareness in the workplace

Developing self-awareness in the workplace is crucial because it allows you to tap into your true potential and cultivate a sense of fulfillment and satisfaction in your career, reminding us of the age-old adage: 'Know thyself.'

When you are self-aware, you have a deep understanding of your strengths, weaknesses, and triggers, enabling you to navigate challenges more effectively and make informed decisions. This awareness also extends to your interactions with colleagues and superiors, as you become more attuned to their emotions and needs.

By being mindful of your own emotions and how they impact others, you can foster better communication, build stronger relationships, and resolve conflicts more constructively. Furthermore, self-awareness enables you to take ownership of your actions and behaviors, allowing you to adapt and grow in response to feedback and criticism.

Ultimately, cultivating self-awareness in the workplace empowers you to become a more effective and empathetic leader, fostering a positive and harmonious work environment for yourself and those around you.

The role of emotional self-awareness in leadership

Discovering and embracing your emotional self-awareness as a leader allows you to effortlessly connect with your team and create a harmonious work environment. By understanding and acknowledging your own emotions, you gain the ability to empathize with others, making you a more effective leader.

When you are aware of your own emotional states, you can manage them in a way that positively influences your team, inspiring them to work together towards a common goal. Additionally, emotional self-awareness allows you to recognize and address any negative emotions that may arise, preventing them from affecting your decision-making or relationships with your team members.

This level of self-awareness also enables you to adapt your leadership style based on the emotional needs of your team, fostering a sense of trust and openness. Ultimately, emotional self-awareness is a vital component of effective leadership, as it allows you to create a supportive and productive work environment where everyone feels valued and understood.

III. Self-Regulation

In this subtopic, you'll explore the concept of self-regulation and its importance in managing your emotions effectively.

Understanding self-regulation involves recognizing your own emotions and being able to control and redirect them in a positive way.

Techniques for self-regulation can include deep breathing exercises, mindfulness practices, and finding healthy outlets for emotions such as journaling or physical activity.

It's important to note that self-regulation may vary in different contexts, such as at work, in relationships, or during stressful situations.

Developing this skill can greatly contribute to your overall emotional intelligence.

Understanding Self-Regulation

Self-regulation is the ability to manage your emotions, thoughts, and behaviors in order to achieve desired outcomes. It involves recognizing your emotional triggers, understanding your thoughts and beliefs, and making deliberate choices in how you respond.

By practicing self-regulation, you can experience benefits such as improved emotional well-being, better decision-making, and stronger relationships with others.

Defining self-regulation

Managing your emotions and impulses is crucial for developing emotional intelligence. Self-regulation, also known as self-control or self-management, refers to the ability to monitor and manage your own thoughts, feelings, and behaviors.

It involves being aware of your emotions, understanding their impact on your actions, and making intentional choices about how to respond. Self-regulation allows you to stay calm in stressful situations, resist impulsive reactions, and maintain focus and concentration.

It requires a deep level of self-awareness and the ability to recognize and regulate your own emotional states. By practicing self-regulation, you can better navigate challenging situations, build healthier relationships, and make more thoughtful decisions.

Remember that self-regulation is a skill that can be developed with practice and mindfulness. Take the time to reflect on your emotions, understand the triggers that cause certain reactions, and consciously choose how to respond in a way that aligns with your values and goals.

The process of self-regulation

Take a moment to reflect and imagine yourself effortlessly navigating through challenging situations with the precision and grace of a tightrope walker, maintaining a balanced and composed demeanor.

Self-regulation is a vital process that allows you to harness your emotions, thoughts, and behaviors in a way that promotes well-being and effective decision-making.

By practicing self-awareness and understanding your triggers, you can better manage your reactions and responses in the face of adversity.

It involves consciously monitoring your emotions, thoughts, and physical sensations, and then employing effective strategies to regulate and modulate them.

This process requires you to identify and acknowledge any negative or harmful emotions, allowing yourself to feel them without judgment, and then intentionally shifting your focus towards more positive and constructive emotions.

By cultivating self-regulation, you can enhance your emotional intelligence and navigate through life's challenges with resilience and grace.

Benefits of self-regulation

Cultivating self-regulation allows you to effectively navigate through challenging situations and make well-informed decisions, resulting in enhanced resilience and graceful adaptation to life's adversities.

By practicing self-regulation, you gain control over your emotions and reactions, allowing you to respond thoughtfully rather than impulsively. This enables you to maintain a sense of calm and composure in the face of stress, which can improve your overall well-being.

Additionally, self-regulation fosters emotional intelligence, allowing you to understand and manage your own emotions as well as empathize with others. This skill is crucial in building strong interpersonal relationships and resolving conflicts peacefully.

Furthermore, self-regulation promotes self-discipline and goal achievement. By managing your impulses and staying focused on your objectives, you can overcome obstacles and achieve long-term success.

Overall, cultivating self-regulation is a powerful tool that empowers you to navigate life's challenges with resilience, make wise decisions, and foster meaningful connections with others.

Techniques for Self-Regulation

When it comes to self-regulation, there are several effective techniques you can employ.

Emotional regulation strategies are essential for managing and controlling your emotions in various situations.

Stress management techniques can help you reduce and cope with the stressors that may arise in your life.

Additionally, incorporating meditation and mindfulness practices into your routine can provide you with the tools to stay grounded and present, enabling you to regulate your emotions more effectively.

Emotional regulation strategies

Emotional regulation strategies can be incredibly useful in managing your emotions and improving your overall well-being. By learning how to regulate your emotions, you can gain a better understanding of yourself and how to respond effectively to different situations.

One strategy is to practice mindfulness, which involves being fully present in the moment and observing your thoughts and feelings without judgment. This can help you become more aware of your emotions and prevent them from overwhelming you.

Another strategy is to engage in self-care activities that promote relaxation and stress reduction, such as exercising, meditating, or spending time in nature. Taking care of yourself physically and mentally can help you build resilience and cope better with challenging emotions.

Additionally, developing healthy coping mechanisms, such as talking to a trusted friend or therapist, can provide you with support and guidance when you're struggling with intense emotions.

It's important to remember that emotional regulation is a skill that takes practice and patience, but with time, it can lead to a more balanced and fulfilling life.

Stress management techniques

To effectively manage stress, you can try incorporating relaxation techniques into your daily routine. These techniques can help you calm your mind and body, reducing the physical and emotional tension that often accompanies stress.

By taking a few moments each day to focus on your breath or release tension in your muscles, you can create a sense of calm and promote a state of relaxation.

Additionally, engaging in activities that you enjoy, such as listening to music, practicing yoga, or taking a walk in nature, can also be effective stress management techniques. These activities can help distract your mind from stressors and provide a sense of pleasure and peace.

Remember, managing stress is an ongoing process, and finding the techniques that work best for you may take some time and experimentation. Be patient with yourself and prioritize self-care as you navigate the challenges of daily life.

Meditation and mindfulness for self-regulation

Meditation and mindfulness are like a soothing breeze that gently guides your thoughts and emotions, allowing you to find inner balance and self-regulation.

In the busy and chaotic world we live in, it's easy to get caught up in the whirlwind of stress and lose sight of ourselves. However, by practicing meditation and mindfulness, you can create a space of stillness within yourself, where you can observe your thoughts and emotions without judgment.

This awareness cultivates a deep sense of self-understanding and helps you develop the ability to regulate your emotions more effectively. Through meditation, you can learn to detach from the constant stream of thoughts and worries, and instead, focus your attention on the present moment.

By doing so, you can cultivate a sense of calm and clarity that allows you to respond to stressful situations with greater composure and resilience. With regular practice, meditation and mindfulness become powerful tools for self-regulation, helping you navigate the ups and downs of life with grace and ease.

Self-Regulation in Different Contexts

In the workplace, self-regulation is crucial for maintaining professionalism and productivity. It involves managing your emotions and reactions to stressful situations, allowing you to respond thoughtfully and constructively.

In relationships, self-regulation plays a vital role in fostering healthy communication and resolving conflicts effectively. By regulating your emotions, you can avoid impulsive reactions and instead respond with empathy and understanding.

Lastly, self-regulation is essential for personal growth as it enables you to identify and manage your thoughts, emotions, and behaviors. By developing this skill, you can make conscious choices that align with your values and goals, leading to personal and professional success.

Self-regulation in the workplace

You can effectively manage your emotions in the workplace by practicing self-regulation. It's crucial to be aware of your emotions and how they may impact your interactions with others.

By taking the time to pause and reflect before reacting, you can avoid potentially harmful or unproductive outcomes. Developing emotional intelligence and understanding your triggers can help you respond in a more controlled and thoughtful manner.

Additionally, setting boundaries and managing your stress levels can contribute to a more positive and harmonious work environment. Remember, self-regulation is a skill that can be learned and improved over time.

By prioritizing your emotional well-being and consciously choosing how to respond, you can cultivate a more productive and fulfilling work experience.

Self-regulation in relationships

Developing the ability to regulate your emotions is like tending a garden in a relationship, nurturing and pruning to maintain a healthy and harmonious connection. Just as a garden requires attention, so do relationships.

It takes effort and self-awareness to regulate your emotions and respond to your partner in a way that promotes understanding and empathy. It means being mindful of your reactions and taking the time to pause and reflect before responding. By doing so, you can prevent unnecessary conflicts and misunderstandings, and instead, create an environment where open communication and emotional connection can thrive.

Self-regulation in relationships also involves setting boundaries and recognizing when it's necessary to express your needs and concerns. It's about finding a balance between expressing your emotions and respecting the emotions of your partner. By actively working on self-regulation, you can foster a deeper level of emotional intelligence, which ultimately strengthens your relationship.

Remember, just as a garden flourishes when nurtured, so does a relationship when emotions are tended to with care and understanding.

Self-regulation for personal growth

Take a moment to reflect on how regulating your emotions can contribute to your personal growth and create a more fulfilling and balanced life.

Self-regulation is a crucial aspect of personal growth as it allows you to navigate through life's challenges with ease and grace. By learning to regulate your emotions, you gain the ability to respond rather than react, making conscious choices that align with your values and goals.

This process requires self-awareness and introspection, allowing you to identify and understand the underlying emotions that drive your thoughts and actions. As you become more skilled at self-regulation, you develop emotional intelligence, which enables you to manage stress, handle conflicts, and maintain healthy relationships.

It also allows you to cultivate a positive mindset, enhance your resilience, and foster personal well-being. Through self-regulation, you can transform your emotional experiences into opportunities for growth, empowering yourself to lead a more fulfilling and balanced life.

IV. Motivation

In this section, we'll explore the role of motivation in emotional intelligence and how it impacts our daily lives. Understanding how motivation influences our emotions can help us navigate challenges more effectively and make informed choices.

We'll also discuss strategies for building and sustaining motivation, as well as how motivation can vary in different areas of life, such as work, relationships, and personal goals.

The Role of Motivation in Emotional Intelligence

When it comes to understanding motivation, you must delve deep into the realm of emotional intelligence.

Intrinsic motivation is an essential component of emotional intelligence, as it springs from within and drives individuals to achieve their goals.

The connection between motivation and goal-setting is crucial, as motivation provides the fuel needed to pursue and accomplish these goals.

Understanding motivation

Motivation, just like a roaring fire, can ignite the deepest passions within you, propelling you towards your greatest achievements. It is the driving force that pushes you to set goals, take action, and persist in the face of challenges.

Understanding motivation is crucial in unlocking your emotional intelligence, as it allows you to tap into your inner desires and aspirations. By understanding what truly motivates you, you can align your actions and decisions with your core values and purpose.

Motivation can come from various sources, such as personal goals, external rewards, or a sense of purpose. It is important to recognize that motivation is not a constant state but can fluctuate over time. By cultivating self-awareness and regularly reassessing your motivations, you can adapt your strategies and stay aligned with your evolving desires.

Remember, motivation is not just about achieving external success, but also about finding fulfillment and joy in the journey towards your goals. So, fuel your motivation, embrace your passions, and let them guide you towards your greatest accomplishments.

Importance of intrinsic motivation

Now that you have a deeper understanding of motivation, let's delve into the importance of intrinsic motivation.

Intrinsic motivation refers to the act of engaging in an activity for the sheer enjoyment and satisfaction it brings, rather than for external rewards or recognition. It's a powerful force that drives us to pursue our passions, explore our creativity, and strive for personal growth.

When you're intrinsically motivated, you're more likely to experience a sense of fulfillment and find greater meaning in your actions. This type of motivation can fuel your perseverance, resilience, and commitment, allowing you to overcome obstacles and achieve long-term success.

By tapping into your intrinsic motivation, you can unlock your true potential and lead a more fulfilling and purposeful life.

Motivation and goal-setting

Imagine setting goals that align with your deepest desires and then feeling motivated to work towards them, knowing that each step you take brings you closer to the life you've always dreamed of.

Motivation and goal-setting go hand in hand, as one fuels the other. When you set goals that truly resonate with your core values and aspirations, you tap into a wellspring of motivation that propels you forward.

It's not just about setting any goal, but about setting meaningful and purposeful goals that ignite a fire within you. By identifying what truly matters to you and what you genuinely want to achieve, you create a clear path towards success.

Motivation acts as the driving force that pushes you to overcome obstacles, persevere through challenges, and stay focused on your goals. As you make progress towards your aspirations, you gain a sense of fulfillment and satisfaction, bolstering your motivation even further.

It becomes a positive feedback loop, where your motivation fuels your actions, and your actions fuel your motivation. So, take the time to reflect on your deepest desires and set goals that align with them. Nurture your motivation, and watch as it propels you towards the life you've always dreamed of.

Building and Sustaining Motivation

In this discussion, we'll explore strategies to enhance your motivation, overcome obstacles that may hinder your motivation, and cultivate a growth mindset.

By implementing effective strategies, such as setting clear goals and creating a positive environment, you can boost your motivation levels.

Additionally, we'll explore ways to overcome common obstacles, such as fear of failure or lack of support, that can often dampen motivation.

Lastly, we'll delve into the importance of cultivating a growth mindset. This involves embracing challenges, learning from setbacks, and believing in your ability to improve.

Strategies to enhance motivation

Boost your motivation by setting clear goals and envisioning yourself achieving them, fueling your drive towards success. One effective strategy to enhance motivation is to break down your goals into smaller, manageable tasks. By doing this, you can create a sense of progress and accomplishment, which will, in turn, motivate you to keep going.

Another strategy is to surround yourself with positive and supportive people who believe in your abilities and goals. Their encouragement and belief in you can boost your motivation and provide a sense of accountability.

Additionally, finding ways to reward yourself along the way can also help enhance motivation. By celebrating small milestones or achievements, you can maintain a positive mindset and continue to strive towards your larger goals.

Finally, it is important to remember that motivation can fluctuate, and it's okay to experience moments of low motivation. During these times, it can be helpful to reflect on your reasons for pursuing your goals and remind yourself of the potential rewards and benefits that await you.

Overcoming obstacles to motivation

Conquering obstacles to motivation can feel like scaling a mountain without any climbing gear. It's a daunting task that requires immense strength and determination. But don't worry, you're not alone in this journey.

Everyone faces obstacles along the way, and it's how you navigate through them that truly matters. One of the first steps to overcoming these obstacles is to identify what's blocking your motivation. Is it fear of failure, lack of confidence, or external pressures? Once you pinpoint the root cause, you can start developing strategies to tackle it head-on.

It's important to remember that motivation isn't a constant state, and it's natural to encounter setbacks. Be kind to yourself during these times and focus on self-care. Surround yourself with a supportive network of friends, family, or mentors who can offer guidance and encouragement.

Break down your goals into smaller, manageable tasks to avoid feeling overwhelmed. Celebrate your achievements along the way, no matter how small they may seem. And most importantly, remember that motivation is something that can be cultivated and nurtured. It may take time, effort, and perseverance, but with the right mindset and strategies, you can overcome any obstacle and unlock your true potential.

Cultivating a growth mindset

Now that you've learned about overcoming obstacles to motivation, let's delve into the importance of cultivating a growth mindset.

A growth mindset is the belief that you have the ability to develop and improve your skills and qualities through dedication and hard work. It's about embracing challenges, seeing failures as opportunities to learn, and persisting in the face of setbacks.

When you have a growth mindset, you understand that intelligence and abilities are not fixed traits, but rather can be developed and expanded upon. This mindset allows you to approach new tasks and challenges with enthusiasm and a willingness to learn, ultimately leading to greater success and fulfillment in your personal and professional life.

So, how can you cultivate a growth mindset?

Motivation in Different Areas of Life

When it comes to motivation in education and learning, you may find yourself needing a boost to stay focused and committed to your studies. Understanding what drives you, whether it's a desire for knowledge, personal growth, or future opportunities, can help you maintain the drive to succeed academically.

In terms of career and professional development, motivation plays a crucial role in pushing you to set goals, seek new opportunities, and continuously improve your skills. It's important to find fulfillment and purpose in your work, as this can fuel your motivation and drive you towards success.

Lastly, motivation in personal relationships is essential for maintaining healthy connections and fostering growth. Whether it's a romantic partnership, friendship, or family bond, finding shared values, goals, and interests can help keep the fire alive and motivate you to invest time and effort into nurturing these relationships.

Motivation in education and learning

Discover the key to unlocking your full potential by understanding the role of motivation in your educational journey and how it shapes your ability to learn.

Motivation plays a crucial role in education and learning, as it's the driving force that pushes you to acquire knowledge and develop new skills. When you're motivated, you're more likely to engage in learning activities, persist through challenges, and strive for excellence.

Motivation can come from various sources, such as intrinsic factors like a genuine interest in the subject matter or extrinsic factors like external rewards or recognition. Understanding what motivates you personally can help you tailor your learning approach and create an environment that fosters your motivation.

Additionally, motivation can be influenced by external factors such as the support and encouragement you receive from teachers, peers, and family members. By recognizing the importance of motivation in education and actively nurturing it, you can enhance your learning experience and achieve academic success.

Remember, motivation isn't a constant state, and it may fluctuate over time. It's essential to cultivate strategies to maintain and boost your motivation, such as setting goals, breaking tasks into manageable chunks, celebrating achievements, and seeking support when needed.

Embrace the power of motivation, and you'll unlock your full potential in your educational journey.

Motivation in career and professional development

Unleash your full potential in your career and professional development by harnessing the power of motivation, driving you to excel and continuously improve.

Motivation plays a crucial role in shaping the trajectory of your career. It acts as the driving force behind your actions, pushing you to set goals, take on challenges, and strive for excellence. Without motivation, it is easy to fall into a state of complacency, where growth and progress become stagnant.

By understanding what motivates you and tapping into that inner drive, you can unlock new levels of success and fulfillment in your professional journey. Motivation not only fuels your ambition but also helps you navigate obstacles and setbacks with resilience and determination. It provides you with the energy and focus needed to overcome challenges, learn from failures, and keep pushing forward.

When you are motivated, you become more proactive in seeking opportunities for growth and development, actively seeking out new skills and knowledge that will enhance your professional capabilities. Motivation also fosters a positive mindset, allowing you to approach your work with enthusiasm and passion. It enables you to find joy and satisfaction in your achievements, leading to increased job satisfaction and overall well-being.

By harnessing the power of motivation, you can unlock your full potential and achieve success in your career and professional development.

Motivation in personal relationships

Motivation plays a pivotal role in shaping the dynamics and longevity of personal relationships, fueling you to invest effort, time, and emotional energy into nurturing and strengthening your connections.

It is the driving force that propels you to actively engage with your partner, family, and friends, and to prioritize their needs and well-being.

Motivation in personal relationships is multifaceted, as it encompasses various aspects such as love, companionship, support, and personal growth.

When you're motivated in your relationships, you're more likely to communicate effectively, resolve conflicts, and show empathy towards your loved ones.

This motivation also helps you overcome challenges, as it encourages you to persevere and work towards maintaining a healthy and fulfilling relationship.

Ultimately, motivation in personal relationships is essential for fostering emotional intimacy, building trust, and creating a strong foundation for a lasting connection.

V. Empathy

In this section, you'll explore the concept of empathy and its importance in emotional intelligence. Understanding empathy involves recognizing and understanding the emotions of others, allowing you to connect with them on a deeper level.

Developing empathy skills can be a transformative process, as it enables you to respond to others with compassion and understanding. Additionally, empathy plays a crucial role in building and maintaining relationships, as it fosters a sense of trust, support, and connection with others.

Understanding Empathy

So, you want to delve into the world of empathy? Well, let's start by defining what empathy is. It's the ability to understand and share the feelings of others. It's about putting yourself in their shoes and truly connecting with their emotions.

Now, empathy comes in various forms. There's cognitive empathy, emotional empathy, and compassionate empathy. Each form offers a unique perspective on the human experience.

And why is empathy so important, you might ask? It's because empathy allows us to build stronger relationships, foster understanding, and create a more compassionate and inclusive society.

Defining empathy

Imagine yourself as a mirror, reflecting the emotions of others and understanding their experiences - that's the essence of empathy, a powerful tool in decoding emotional intelligence.

When you truly empathize with someone, you're able to put yourself in their shoes and see the world through their eyes. It goes beyond just sympathizing or feeling sorry for someone; it involves actively listening, validating their emotions, and showing genuine care and understanding.

Empathy allows you to connect with others on a deeper level, breaking down barriers and fostering trust and compassion. It's an important skill to have in decoding emotional intelligence because it helps you decode the underlying emotions and motivations behind someone's actions.

By understanding and acknowledging another person's feelings, you can gain insights into their thought processes and make more informed decisions.

So, next time you find yourself in a situation where someone is expressing their emotions, try to step into their shoes and truly empathize with them. You may be surprised at the depth of connection and understanding that can be achieved.

Different types of empathy

To truly connect with others and foster trust and compassion, it's important to understand the different types of empathy.

Empathy is not a one-size-fits-all concept; it encompasses various forms that allow us to relate to and understand others' experiences.

Cognitive empathy, for instance, involves understanding someone's perspective and emotions without necessarily sharing those feelings. This type of empathy allows us to put ourselves in someone else's shoes and see the world from their point of view.

Emotional empathy, on the other hand, involves feeling the same emotions as another person, almost as if we're experiencing their feelings ourselves. This type of empathy enables us to connect on a deeper emotional level, but it also puts us at risk of becoming overwhelmed by others' emotions.

Lastly, compassionate empathy combines both cognitive and emotional empathy, allowing us to understand and share others' emotions while also taking action to help and support them.

By recognizing and cultivating these different types of empathy, we can enhance our ability to connect with others, build stronger relationships, and create a more empathetic and compassionate world.

The importance of empathy

Understanding and practicing empathy allows you to connect with others on a deeper level, fostering trust and compassion. But how can you truly comprehend the impact empathy has on your relationships and the world around you?

Empathy is crucial because it helps you understand and share the feelings of others, enabling you to provide support and comfort. By putting yourself in someone else's shoes, you can gain insight into their experiences and perspectives, strengthening your bond and creating a sense of belonging.

Empathy also promotes effective communication and conflict resolution, as it allows you to listen and validate the emotions of others, fostering understanding and cooperation.

Additionally, empathy plays a vital role in creating a more compassionate and inclusive society. When you empathize with others, you're more likely to take action to address social issues and advocate for change. Through empathy, you can break down barriers, bridge gaps, and foster a sense of unity among diverse individuals.

Ultimately, empathy is a powerful tool that not only enhances your personal relationships but also has the potential to transform the world around you, promoting understanding, acceptance, and love.

Developing Empathy Skills

When it comes to developing empathy skills, there are three key points to focus on.

Firstly, cultivating active listening skills is crucial in truly understanding and connecting with others. By fully engaging in conversations and paying attention to both verbal and non-verbal cues, you can better comprehend someone's emotions and experiences.

Secondly, practicing perspective-taking allows you to step into someone else's shoes and see the world through their eyes. This helps foster empathy by allowing you to understand their unique circumstances and challenges.

Lastly, building emotional intelligence through empathy is essential. By recognizing and acknowledging your own emotions, as well as those of others, you can cultivate a deeper sense of empathy and strengthen your relationships.

Cultivating active listening skills

Developing active listening skills can greatly enhance your ability to connect with others on a deeper level, allowing you to truly understand their emotions and experiences.

When you actively listen to someone, you're fully present in the conversation, giving them your undivided attention. This means putting aside distractions and focusing on what the other person is saying, both verbally and non-verbally.

By doing so, you're able to pick up on subtle cues, such as tone of voice, facial expressions, and body language, which can provide valuable insight into their emotions.

Additionally, active listening involves not only hearing the words being spoken but also understanding the underlying emotions and intentions behind them. This requires empathy and the ability to put yourself in the other person's shoes.

By cultivating active listening skills, you can create a safe and supportive environment for others to express themselves, fostering deeper connections and promoting emotional well-being.

Practicing perspective-taking

To truly connect with others on a deeper level, you must hone your ability to practice perspective-taking, allowing you to see the world through their eyes and gain a greater understanding of their experiences and emotions.

When you actively engage in perspective-taking, you open yourself up to a whole new level of empathy and compassion. It requires you to set aside your own biases and preconceptions, and truly listen to what the other person is saying.

By doing so, you not only validate their feelings and experiences, but you also create a safe space for them to open up and express themselves. Perspective-taking is a powerful tool that allows you to build trust and create meaningful connections with others.

It helps you to break down barriers and bridge the gap between different perspectives, fostering a sense of unity and understanding. So the next time you find yourself in a conversation, challenge yourself to actively practice perspective-taking.

Listen with an open mind and an open heart, and watch as your relationships deepen and flourish.

Building emotional intelligence through empathy

Practicing empathy allows you to step into someone else's shoes and truly understand their feelings and experiences, creating a deeper connection. By actively listening to others and trying to understand their perspective, you can develop a greater sense of emotional intelligence.

Empathy involves not only recognizing and acknowledging someone's emotions, but also validating their experiences. It requires setting aside your own biases and judgments, and instead focusing on truly understanding and empathizing with the other person.

When you practice empathy, you show others that you genuinely care about their feelings and are willing to support them. This builds trust and fosters stronger relationships, as people feel heard and understood.

Furthermore, empathy helps you to develop a broader understanding of the world around you, as you gain insight into different perspectives and experiences. It allows you to challenge your own assumptions and biases, leading to personal growth and a more open-minded approach to life.

Overall, building emotional intelligence through empathy enables you to connect with others on a deeper level, fostering understanding and compassion in both personal and professional relationships.

Empathy in Relationships

When it comes to romantic relationships, empathy plays a crucial role in creating a strong and healthy connection with your partner.

Understanding and validating each other's emotions can foster a deeper level of intimacy and trust.

In family relationships, empathy is essential for maintaining harmony and resolving conflicts.

Being able to put yourself in the shoes of your family members can help you better understand their perspectives and find common ground.

Lastly, empathy is equally important in friendships and social connections.

By showing empathy towards others, you can build meaningful and supportive relationships, as well as create a sense of belonging and acceptance.

Empathy in romantic relationships

Understanding and feeling your partner's emotions is crucial for building a deep and meaningful connection in a romantic relationship. Empathy plays a significant role in fostering understanding and emotional intimacy between partners.

It involves being able to put yourself in your partner's shoes, truly understanding their feelings, and responding with compassion and support. When you empathize with your partner, you create a safe space for them to express themselves openly and honestly, knowing that their emotions will be acknowledged and validated.

This level of emotional attunement allows you to navigate conflicts and challenges more effectively, as you are able to truly understand each other's perspectives. It also deepens the bond between you, as you demonstrate your willingness to be there for each other in both joyful and difficult moments.

Empathy in romantic relationships is a powerful tool that can strengthen your connection and help you create a loving and lasting partnership.

Empathy in family relationships

Empathy can create profound connections, fostering love and understanding within family relationships, where support and compassion are paramount.

When you empathize with your family members, you're able to truly understand their emotions and experiences, allowing you to offer support and comfort in times of need.

By putting yourself in their shoes, you can gain insight into their perspective and develop a deeper bond.

Empathy helps you to validate their feelings and lets them know that they're not alone in their struggles.

It enables you to communicate effectively and resolve conflicts in a respectful and understanding manner.

When empathy is present in family relationships, it creates a safe and nurturing environment where everyone feels heard, valued, and loved.

It is through empathy that we can build stronger and more meaningful connections with our family members, fostering a sense of belonging and togetherness.

Empathy in friendships and social connections

Developing empathy in friendships and social connections allows you to form deeper bonds and create a sense of belonging in your life.

When you can empathize with others, you're able to understand their emotions and experiences on a deeper level. It gives you the ability to put yourself in their shoes and truly connect with them.

This connection not only strengthens your relationships but also allows you to provide support and comfort when needed.

Empathy in friendships and social connections is essential for fostering trust, understanding, and compassion. It enables you to navigate conflicts and disagreements with empathy, leading to more meaningful and fulfilling relationships.

By cultivating empathy, you can create a safe and supportive space for yourself and others, where everyone feels seen, heard, and valued.

VI. Social Skills

When it comes to emotional intelligence, social skills play a crucial role in navigating various situations and building strong relationships.

Developing effective social skills involves understanding and managing emotions, active listening, and effective communication.

Additionally, it's important to recognize that social skills are not a one-size-fits-all approach; they can vary depending on the setting and the people involved.

The Role of Social Skills in Emotional Intelligence

So, you want to understand the role of social skills in emotional intelligence? Well, let's start by defining what social skills actually are.

Social skills refer to the ability to effectively communicate, interact, and build relationships with others. They play a crucial role in emotional intelligence because they enable individuals to navigate social situations and understand the emotions of those around them.

Now, let's talk about why effective social skills are so important. When you possess strong social skills, you're better equipped to establish and maintain meaningful connections with others. This not only enhances your personal relationships, but it also allows you to navigate various social and professional settings with ease. In other words, having good social skills can greatly contribute to your overall success and well-being.

Lastly, it's important to recognize the direct link between social skills and personal success. When you possess strong social skills, you're more likely to excel in both your personal and professional life. Effective communication, empathy, and the ability to understand and manage emotions are all essential components of social skills that can lead to greater personal achievements and fulfillment. So, honing your social skills is definitely worth the effort!

Defining social skills

Don't you just love it when your social skills are impeccable and everyone wants to be around you?

Having strong social skills is a key component of emotional intelligence, allowing you to navigate social situations with ease and build meaningful connections with others.

Social skills encompass a range of abilities, including effective communication, active listening, empathy, and conflict resolution.

When you possess these skills, you become adept at understanding and responding to the emotions and needs of those around you.

People are naturally drawn to individuals who are able to engage in meaningful conversations, show genuine interest, and make others feel valued.

Developing your social skills not only enhances your emotional intelligence but also enriches your personal and professional relationships.

So, why not strive to improve your social skills and experience the joy of connecting with others on a deeper level?

The importance of effective social skills

Imagine how much more enjoyable and fulfilling your interactions with others could be if you honed your social skills to perfection.

Effective social skills play a crucial role in our everyday lives, shaping the quality of our relationships, both personal and professional.

When you possess strong social skills, you're able to navigate social situations with ease, communicate effectively, and build meaningful connections with others.

You become adept at understanding nonverbal cues, empathizing with others, and resolving conflicts in a constructive manner.

By mastering these skills, you open yourself up to a world of opportunities, as you're more likely to succeed in your career, form lasting friendships, and cultivate healthy romantic relationships.

Moreover, effective social skills contribute to your overall emotional well-being, reducing stress and enhancing your sense of belonging and fulfillment.

So take the time to invest in developing your social skills, as they're the key to unlocking a more rewarding and enriching social life.

Social skills and personal success

Developing strong social skills is the key to unlocking a world of personal success, allowing you to effortlessly navigate social interactions, build meaningful connections, and open up a wealth of opportunities.

By honing your ability to communicate effectively, understand others' emotions, and adapt to different social situations, you can enhance your emotional intelligence and greatly improve your personal and professional relationships.

When you possess strong social skills, you become more adept at reading nonverbal cues, understanding the needs and motivations of others, and resolving conflicts in a constructive manner. This not only leads to more satisfying interactions but also enables you to build a network of supportive individuals who can help you achieve your goals.

Moreover, having strong social skills can significantly boost your self-confidence and overall well-being, as you navigate through life with a greater sense of ease and understanding.

So, invest time and effort into developing your social skills, as they are integral to your personal success and fulfillment.

Developing Effective Social Skills

When it comes to developing effective social skills, you need to focus on communication skills for building relationships, conflict resolution and negotiation, and building rapport and networking.

By honing your communication skills, you can better understand and connect with others, creating stronger relationships.

Conflict resolution and negotiation skills are crucial for navigating difficult situations and finding mutually beneficial solutions.

Finally, building rapport and networking can open doors to new opportunities and connections, allowing you to expand your social circle and professional network.

Embracing these skills will not only enhance your emotional intelligence but also help you thrive in both personal and professional aspects of your life.

Communication skills for building relationships

Effective communication skills are essential for establishing and nurturing strong relationships. When it comes to building relationships, being able to effectively communicate with others is crucial. It's not just about what you say, but how you say it and how you listen.

By using active listening skills, you show that you're truly interested in what the other person has to say and value their perspective. This can help create a sense of trust and understanding, which are vital for any relationship to thrive.

Additionally, being able to express your thoughts and emotions clearly and respectfully can prevent misunderstandings and conflicts.

It allows both parties to openly share their feelings and concerns, fostering a deeper connection and resolving any issues that may arise.

In any relationship, whether it's personal or professional, effective communication skills play a significant role in building trust, establishing rapport, and maintaining a healthy and harmonious connection.

So take the time to hone your communication skills, practice active listening, and be mindful of how you express yourself, as it can make all the difference in building lasting and meaningful relationships.

Conflict resolution and negotiation

Mastering conflict resolution and negotiation skills is essential for successfully navigating through challenging situations and finding mutually beneficial solutions.

In order to effectively resolve conflicts, it's important to approach the situation with a calm and open mindset. By actively listening to the concerns and perspectives of all parties involved, you can gain a deeper understanding of the underlying issues and emotions driving the conflict.

This empathetic approach allows you to find common ground and work towards a resolution that satisfies everyone's needs.

Additionally, effective negotiation skills are crucial in finding compromises and reaching mutually beneficial agreements. By being assertive yet respectful, you can advocate for your own interests while also considering the needs and desires of the other party.

This analytical and insightful approach to conflict resolution and negotiation can lead to improved relationships, increased trust, and long-lasting solutions.

Building rapport and networking

You may think that building rapport and networking is just a waste of time, but little do you know that it can open doors to countless opportunities and connections that can greatly benefit your personal and professional life.

Building rapport is about establishing a genuine connection with others, creating a sense of trust and understanding. When you take the time to build rapport, you show others that you value them and their opinions, which can lead to stronger relationships and collaborations.

Networking, on the other hand, allows you to expand your circle of influence and connect with individuals who can offer unique perspectives and opportunities. By actively engaging in networking events and cultivating relationships with people from different backgrounds and industries, you can gain valuable insights, knowledge, and support.

Ultimately, building rapport and networking are essential skills for success in today's interconnected world. So, don't underestimate their power and start investing in these practices to unlock a wealth of possibilities.

Social Skills in Different Settings

In the workplace, social skills are essential for building relationships with colleagues, collaborating effectively, and advancing your career.

Developing strong social skills in community and social interactions allows you to navigate social situations with ease, connect with others, and contribute positively to your community.

In leadership and team dynamics, social skills are vital for effective communication, fostering a positive work environment, and leading a team towards shared goals.

Remember, honing your social skills in these different settings can greatly enhance your success and satisfaction in both your personal and professional life.

Social skills in the workplace

Developing strong social skills is essential for success in the workplace, as they allow you to effectively communicate, collaborate, and build positive relationships with your colleagues.

In a professional setting, being able to connect with others on a personal level can greatly enhance your ability to work as part of a team and accomplish common goals.

Good social skills can also help you navigate conflicts and resolve issues in a constructive manner, fostering a positive work environment.

By understanding and empathizing with the emotions and perspectives of your coworkers, you can create a supportive and inclusive workplace culture where everyone feels valued and heard.

Furthermore, strong social skills can also enhance your leadership abilities, as effective leaders are often those who can inspire and motivate their team members.

By developing your social intelligence, you can build trust, gain respect, and ultimately achieve greater success in your career.

Social skills in community and social interactions

Now that you've learned about the importance of social skills in the workplace, let's delve into how these skills play a crucial role in community and social interactions.

In your daily life, whether you're at a social gathering, engaging in a group activity, or simply interacting with friends and family, your social skills are instrumental in forming meaningful connections and fostering positive relationships.

These skills enable you to effectively communicate, empathize, and understand others, allowing you to navigate various social situations with confidence and ease. By honing your social skills, you not only enhance your own well-being but also contribute to the overall harmony and cohesion of your community.

So, let's explore how developing and applying these skills can enrich your social interactions and create a more empathetic and inclusive environment for everyone.

Social skills in leadership and team dynamics

Enhancing your social skills in leadership and team dynamics can greatly improve your ability to collaborate and inspire others, leading to a 33% increase in team productivity.

When you have strong social skills, you're able to effectively communicate your vision, motivate your team, and create a positive work environment.

By understanding the dynamics of teamwork and the importance of emotional intelligence, you can establish trust and build strong relationships with your team members. This allows you to effectively delegate tasks, resolve conflicts, and foster a sense of unity within the group.

Additionally, your ability to empathize with others and understand their needs and concerns will enable you to address any issues that may arise and find innovative solutions.

By developing your social skills, you'll become a more effective leader, capable of inspiring and guiding your team towards success.

VII. Emotional Intelligence and Resilience

In this section, we'll explore the topic of emotional intelligence and resilience.

Understanding resilience is key to navigating life's challenges and setbacks. By building emotional intelligence, you can develop the tools and skills needed to bounce back from adversity and overcome obstacles.

Whether it's facing personal or professional challenges, resilience plays a crucial role in maintaining your well-being and achieving success.

Understanding Resilience

Resilience is a key component of emotional intelligence, and it refers to your ability to bounce back from setbacks and challenges in life.

It is made up of various components, including self-awareness, self-regulation, and optimism.

By developing resilience, you can not only better manage stress and adversity but also build stronger relationships and achieve greater success in various areas of your life.

Definition and components of resilience

Despite life's challenges, resilience allows you to bounce back and navigate the twists and turns with grace and strength.

Resilience can be defined as the ability to adapt and recover from adversity, setbacks, and difficult situations. It's not just about being tough or having a thick skin; rather, it involves a complex set of emotional, cognitive, and behavioral components.

Emotionally, resilience involves the ability to regulate and cope with negative emotions, such as stress, anxiety, and sadness. It requires self-awareness and the ability to identify and understand your emotions.

Cognitively, resilience involves having a positive mindset and the ability to reframe and find meaning in challenging situations. It involves having a sense of optimism, hope, and belief in your own ability to overcome obstacles.

Behaviorally, resilience involves taking action and problem-solving. It means being proactive and seeking support from others when needed.

Resilience is not a fixed trait, but rather a skill that can be developed and strengthened through practice and experience. By cultivating resilience, you can not only bounce back from adversity but also thrive and grow in the face of challenges.

The connection between emotional intelligence and resilience

Picture yourself navigating life's challenges with grace and strength, bouncing back from setbacks and difficult situations.

Emotional intelligence plays a crucial role in building resilience, allowing individuals to effectively cope with adversity and bounce back from difficult experiences.

When you possess a high level of emotional intelligence, you're able to recognize and understand your own emotions, as well as the emotions of others.

This self-awareness and empathy enable you to regulate your emotions and respond to challenging situations in a more constructive manner.

By developing emotional intelligence, you can cultivate a positive mindset, build strong relationships, and effectively manage stress and adversity.

This heightened emotional intelligence empowers you to adapt to change, learn from failures, and view setbacks as opportunities for growth.

Through the connection between emotional intelligence and resilience, you can enhance your ability to overcome obstacles and thrive in the face of adversity.

Benefits of developing resilience

One of the advantages of developing resilience is that it allows you to bounce back from setbacks and difficult situations, creating a sense of inner strength and determination.

When you have resilience, you are better equipped to handle challenges and obstacles that come your way. Rather than getting knocked down and staying down, you have the ability to rise above and keep moving forward.

Developing resilience also helps you to develop a positive mindset and perspective. Instead of dwelling on the negatives, you are able to focus on finding solutions and learning from your experiences.

This ability to adapt and grow in the face of adversity is crucial for personal and professional success.

Resilience also promotes emotional well-being. When you are resilient, you have a greater ability to manage stress and cope with difficult emotions. You're more likely to have a positive outlook on life and maintain healthy relationships.

Overall, developing resilience is an essential skill that can greatly enhance your ability to navigate life's challenges and thrive in the face of adversity.

Building Emotional Intelligence for Resilience

In order to enhance your emotional intelligence for resilience, it's important to employ certain strategies.

These strategies can include developing self-awareness, practicing empathy, and understanding others' emotions.

Learning effective communication skills.

By cultivating inner strength and resilience, you can better navigate through challenging situations and bounce back from setbacks with greater ease and confidence.

Strategies to enhance emotional intelligence for resilience

Imagine how much stronger and more resilient you can become by implementing strategies to enhance your emotional intelligence. By actively working on improving your emotional intelligence, you can develop a deeper understanding of your own emotions and those of others, allowing you to navigate challenging situations with greater ease.

One strategy to enhance emotional intelligence is to practice self-awareness by regularly checking in with yourself and acknowledging your emotions without judgment. This can help you gain insight into your own triggers and reactions, enabling you to respond in a more composed and thoughtful manner.

Additionally, developing empathy towards others can greatly enhance your emotional intelligence. By putting yourself in someone else's shoes and truly understanding their perspective, you can build stronger connections and foster healthier relationships.

Finally, learning effective communication skills can also contribute to your emotional intelligence. By expressing your emotions clearly and assertively, while also actively listening to others, you can avoid misunderstandings and resolve conflicts more effectively.

By implementing these strategies and continuously working on enhancing your emotional intelligence, you can cultivate resilience and become better equipped to handle life's challenges.

Cultivating inner strength and resilience

Harnessing your inner strength and resilience is as easy as pie, or so they say, but little do they know the true power that lies within you.

Cultivating inner strength and resilience is not a simple task; it requires dedication, self-reflection, and a deep understanding of oneself.

It's about acknowledging your emotions, both positive and negative, and learning how to navigate through them with grace and wisdom.

It's about embracing challenges as opportunities for growth and using setbacks as stepping stones towards success.

It's about finding your center amidst the chaos and having the courage to face adversity head-on.

Inner strength and resilience are not innate qualities that some are born with; they're skills that can be developed and honed over time.

It requires a commitment to self-care, self-awareness, and self-compassion.

By cultivating these qualities, you can tap into your true potential and become a force to be reckoned with.

So, don't underestimate the power that lies within you.

Embrace it, nurture it, and watch yourself grow.

Emotional intelligence and bouncing back from setbacks

Tap into your inner resilience and rise above setbacks by understanding and navigating through your emotions with grace and wisdom.

Life is full of unexpected challenges and disappointments, but it's how we choose to respond to these setbacks that truly defines our character.

Emotional intelligence plays a crucial role in our ability to bounce back and overcome obstacles. By developing a deep understanding of our emotions and learning how to manage them effectively, we can regain control of our lives and move forward with confidence.

It's important to acknowledge and honor our feelings, allowing ourselves to experience them fully without judgment or resistance. This self-awareness allows us to identify the root causes of our setbacks and make conscious choices about how we want to respond.

With practice, we can cultivate a sense of resilience that enables us to bounce back stronger than ever before. Remember, setbacks are not permanent roadblocks, but rather opportunities for growth and learning. Embrace them with an open heart and a curious mind, and you'll discover the strength within you to overcome any adversity that comes your way.

Resilience in Different Life Challenges

When faced with stressful and adverse situations, you possess the remarkable ability to bounce back and overcome challenges.

Your resilience shines through as you navigate through grief and loss, finding strength and healing in the midst of pain.

You demonstrate resilience as you adapt and embrace change, skillfully maneuvering through life's transitions with grace and determination.

—Resilience in times of stress and adversity

Despite facing numerous challenges, individuals with high emotional intelligence have the ability to bounce back like a rubber ball, demonstrating resilience in times of stress and adversity.

When life throws its curveballs, these individuals possess the remarkable capacity to navigate through the stormy waters and come out stronger on the other side.

They understand that stress and adversity are inevitable parts of life, and instead of letting them consume their spirit, they choose to view these challenges as opportunities for growth and self-discovery.

They approach difficult situations with a sense of determination and optimism, knowing that setbacks are not permanent and that they have the power to overcome them.

This resilience is not born out of ignorance or denial of emotions, but rather an acknowledgement and understanding of them.

These emotionally intelligent individuals are in tune with their own emotions and are able to effectively manage them, allowing them to remain calm and composed even in the face of adversity.

They also possess a strong sense of empathy, which enables them to connect with others on a deeper level and provide support during difficult times.

Their ability to stay grounded and maintain a positive outlook in the midst of stress is not only beneficial for their own well-being, but also inspires those around them to do the same.

In a world that can often be overwhelming and unpredictable, resilience in times of stress and adversity is a valuable trait that allows individuals to not only survive, but thrive.

Resilience in grief and loss

In the face of heart-wrenching grief and devastating loss, you, as a person with high emotional intelligence, possess an extraordinary ability to rise above the pain and find strength in the depths of your sorrow.

It is during these challenging times that your resilience shines through, allowing you to navigate the turbulent waves of emotions with grace and understanding.

You understand that grief is a natural part of the human experience and that it's okay to feel a range of emotions, from anger to sadness, as you mourn your loss.

Rather than suppressing these feelings, you embrace them, allowing yourself to fully process and heal.

Your emotional intelligence allows you to tap into your inner strength and find solace in memories, relationships, and the support of others.

You recognize that grief is not a linear journey, but a process that takes time and patience.

Through it all, you emerge stronger, more compassionate, and more resilient, ready to face life's challenges with a renewed sense of purpose and understanding.

Resilience in navigating change and transitions

Amidst the winds of change and the shifting tides of transitions, your ability to adapt and find strength in the unknown becomes a beacon of resilience, guiding you through uncharted waters.

Change and transitions can be both exciting and daunting, as they often bring uncertainty and challenges. However, it's in these moments that your emotional intelligence plays a crucial role. By acknowledging and accepting the emotions that arise during these times, you can better navigate the waves of change.

Understanding that it's normal to feel a mix of excitement, fear, and even sadness allows you to embrace the process and approach it with a sense of curiosity and openness. Through this lens, you can uncover new opportunities and possibilities that may not have been visible before.

Resilience in navigating change and transitions is about staying grounded in your core values and beliefs while remaining flexible and adaptable. It requires a deep understanding of yourself and your emotions, as well as the ability to lean on your support system and seek guidance when needed.

Remember, resilience isn't about avoiding or suppressing emotions, but rather about acknowledging and harnessing them to propel you forward. So, as you face the unknown, trust in your ability to navigate the uncharted waters and find strength in the process of change.

VIII. Emotional Intelligence and Emotional Well-Being

In this section, we'll explore the link between emotional intelligence and emotional well-being. We'll also discuss the important role of self-care in developing emotional intelligence. Understanding and managing our emotions can greatly impact our overall happiness and satisfaction in life. By developing our emotional intelligence skills, we can cultivate a greater sense of self-awareness, empathy, and resilience. This, in turn, leads to a more fulfilling and contented life.

The Link between Emotional Intelligence and Emotional Well-Being

Emotional intelligence plays a significant role in predicting your emotional well-being. By understanding and managing your emotions effectively, you're better equipped to handle life's challenges and maintain a positive mental state.

Additionally, emotional intelligence directly affects your mental health. It enables you to navigate through stress, build resilience, and foster healthier relationships.

To improve your emotional well-being, focus on enhancing your emotional intelligence. Practice self-awareness, empathy, and effective communication skills. With these strategies, you can cultivate a greater sense of emotional well-being and lead a more fulfilling life.

Emotional intelligence as a predictor of emotional well-being

Picture yourself in a world where understanding and managing your emotions is the key to unlocking a life of emotional well-being. Imagine being able to accurately perceive and interpret your own emotions and those of others, and using that knowledge to navigate through life's challenges with ease.

This is the power of emotional intelligence. Research has shown that individuals with high emotional intelligence are more likely to experience higher levels of emotional well-being. Why is this the case? Well, emotional intelligence allows you to effectively cope with stress, regulate your emotions, and maintain positive relationships.

By understanding and managing your emotions, you can better handle difficult situations, bounce back from setbacks, and build strong connections with others. Emotional intelligence is like a compass that guides you towards emotional well-being, helping you to navigate the ups and downs of life with resilience and grace.

So, take a moment to reflect on your own emotional intelligence and how it impacts your emotional well-being. Are there areas where you can improve? Remember, emotional intelligence is a skill that can be developed, and by doing so, you can unlock a world of emotional well-being.

How emotional intelligence affects mental health

Imagine a world where understanding and managing your emotions is the key to unlocking a life of mental well-being, enabling you to navigate through life's challenges with ease.

Emotional intelligence plays a crucial role in our mental health, as it allows us to recognize, understand, and regulate our own emotions, as well as empathize with others.

When we have a high level of emotional intelligence, we are better equipped to handle stress, anxiety, and depression, as we can effectively identify and address the underlying emotions causing these issues.

By being aware of our emotions and understanding their impact on our mental health, we can develop healthier coping mechanisms and make informed decisions that promote our overall well-being.

Additionally, emotional intelligence helps us build stronger relationships and communicate effectively, reducing conflict and fostering a supportive environment.

In this way, emotional intelligence acts as a protective factor, shielding us from the negative effects of mental health issues and enhancing our overall resilience and happiness.

Strategies for improving emotional well-being through emotional intelligence

Now that you understand how emotional intelligence affects your mental health, it's time to explore strategies for improving your emotional well-being through emotional intelligence.

By developing your emotional intelligence, you can gain a better understanding of your own emotions and those of others, which can lead to healthier relationships and a more fulfilling life.

One key strategy is to practice self-awareness by openly acknowledging your emotions and recognizing how they impact your thoughts and behaviors.

Additionally, learning to regulate your emotions can help you manage stress and prevent negative emotions from overwhelming you.

By effectively communicating and empathizing with others, you can also strengthen your relationships and build a support network that promotes emotional well-being.

By incorporating these strategies into your daily life, you can enhance your emotional intelligence and enjoy the benefits of improved emotional well-being.

Self-Care and Emotional Intelligence

Taking care of yourself is crucial for your emotional well-being.

Self-care practices not only help you relax and recharge, but they also enhance your emotional intelligence.

By engaging in activities such as mindfulness meditation, journaling, and seeking support from loved ones, you can integrate emotional intelligence into your self-care routine.

You can develop a deeper understanding of your emotions and how to manage them effectively.

Importance of self-care for emotional well-being

To truly enhance your emotional well-being, it's essential that you prioritize self-care. Taking care of yourself isn't a luxury, but a necessity in today's fast-paced and demanding world.

When you make self-care a priority, you're giving yourself the time and space to recharge, rejuvenate, and heal. It's through self-care that you can replenish your emotional resources, manage stress, and cultivate a deep sense of self-awareness.

By engaging in activities that bring you joy, practicing mindfulness and self-reflection, and setting healthy boundaries, you're taking proactive steps towards nurturing your emotional well-being.

Remember, self-care isn't selfish; it's an act of self-love and self-respect. So, make it a habit to carve out time for yourself, to listen to your needs, and to prioritize your emotional well-being.

Self-care practices that enhance emotional intelligence

Make sure you don't neglect yourself because self-care practices are like emotional superpowers that boost your understanding of others and make you an empathy ninja.

Taking time for yourself and engaging in self-care activities can significantly enhance your emotional intelligence.

When you prioritize self-care, you're giving yourself the opportunity to recharge, reflect, and process your own emotions. This self-reflection allows you to gain a deeper understanding of your own emotional landscape, making it easier for you to empathize with others.

By practicing self-care, you're also showing yourself love and compassion, which in turn allows you to extend that same love and compassion to those around you.

Whether it's through activities like meditation, journaling, exercise, or spending time in nature, self-care practices help you develop a strong foundation of emotional intelligence, enabling you to navigate relationships with greater sensitivity and understanding.

So, make self-care a priority and watch as your emotional intelligence grows, making you an empathy ninja in your interactions with others.

Integrating emotional intelligence into a self-care routine

When you incorporate emotional intelligence into your self-care routine, you unlock a powerful tool for understanding and connecting with others on a deeper level. By prioritizing your emotional well-being and actively working on developing your emotional intelligence, you can enhance your ability to navigate relationships and handle challenging situations with grace and empathy.

Integrating emotional intelligence into your self-care routine involves recognizing and acknowledging your own emotions, as well as actively seeking to understand the emotions of others. This can be done through practices such as mindfulness, journaling, and therapy, which allow you to explore and process your emotions in a safe and supportive environment.

Additionally, engaging in activities that promote self-reflection and self-awareness, such as meditation or introspective exercises, can further deepen your emotional intelligence. As you continue to incorporate emotional intelligence into your self-care routine, you'll find that you not only become more attuned to your own emotions but also better equipped to empathize with and support others.

This increased understanding and connection can lead to more fulfilling relationships, improved communication, and a greater sense of overall well-being.

Emotional Intelligence and Happiness

When it comes to happiness, emotional intelligence plays a crucial role in your overall well-being.

Understanding and managing your emotions effectively can lead to greater happiness and satisfaction in life.

By cultivating emotional intelligence, you can develop strategies to navigate challenging situations, build stronger relationships, and find balance and fulfillment in your daily life.

The role of emotional intelligence in happiness

Emotional intelligence plays a crucial role in our overall happiness. When we're able to understand and manage our own emotions effectively, we create a positive environment within ourselves that fosters happiness.

By being aware of our emotions and recognizing how they influence our thoughts and behaviors, we gain the power to make conscious choices that promote happiness.

Additionally, emotional intelligence allows us to empathize with others, understand their emotions, and build strong, meaningful relationships. When we can connect with others on an emotional level, we create a support system that enhances our well-being and contributes to our overall happiness.

Developing and honing our emotional intelligence skills is therefore essential for cultivating a happier and more fulfilling life.

Strategies for cultivating happiness through emotional intelligence

Now that you understand the significant role emotional intelligence plays in our happiness, it's time to explore the strategies for cultivating happiness through emotional intelligence.

You may be wondering, what can I do to develop my emotional intelligence and ultimately increase my happiness? Well, the good news is that there are several practical steps you can take.

First, start by becoming more self-aware. Pay attention to your emotions and how they impact your thoughts and actions. This self-reflection will allow you to better understand your triggers and patterns.

Next, focus on developing your empathy skills. Try to put yourself in others' shoes and understand their emotions and perspectives. This will not only enhance your relationships but also foster a deeper sense of connection and understanding.

Additionally, practice emotional regulation. Learn to identify and manage your emotions effectively, rather than letting them control you.

Finally, seek out opportunities for growth and learning. Embrace challenges and setbacks as opportunities for self-improvement and personal development.

By implementing these strategies, you can cultivate happiness through emotional intelligence and lead a more fulfilling life.

Finding balance and fulfillment through emotional intelligence

To achieve balance and fulfillment, you can harness the power of emotional intelligence by developing a deep understanding of your own emotions and using that knowledge to navigate your life with clarity and purpose.

By becoming aware of your emotions and their underlying causes, you can make informed choices that align with your values and goals. Emotional intelligence allows you to recognize when you're feeling overwhelmed or out of balance and empowers you to take the necessary steps to restore equilibrium.

It enables you to identify what brings you joy and fulfillment and prioritize those aspects in your life. Through emotional intelligence, you can cultivate self-compassion and self-care, recognizing that your emotional well-being is essential for overall happiness and success.

By practicing empathy and understanding towards others, emotional intelligence fosters stronger relationships and deeper connections. It allows you to communicate effectively, resolve conflicts, and build trust.

Ultimately, emotional intelligence empowers you to lead a more balanced and fulfilling life, where you can navigate challenges with resilience and find greater satisfaction in your personal and professional endeavors.

IX. Emotional Intelligence in Parenting

When it comes to parenting, emotional intelligence plays a crucial role in raising well-rounded children.

As a parent, you have the opportunity to nurture your child's emotional intelligence by providing a supportive and empathetic environment.

Additionally, your own level of emotional intelligence can greatly impact how you navigate the challenges that come with parenting.

Emotional Intelligence and Parenting: An Overview

If you want to be an effective parent, it's important to understand the connection between emotional intelligence and parenting.

Emotional intelligence plays a crucial role in children's development. It helps them understand and manage their own emotions, as well as empathize with others.

Additionally, your own emotional intelligence as a parent can greatly impact your children's emotional well-being and how they navigate their own emotions in the future.

Understanding the connection between emotional intelligence and effective parenting

By harnessing your emotional intelligence, you can become a more effective parent. Understanding the connection between emotional intelligence and effective parenting is crucial in building a strong and healthy relationship with your child.

When you are aware of your own emotions and can regulate them effectively, you're better able to respond to your child's emotional needs. By being empathetic and understanding, you can create a safe and nurturing environment where your child feels valued and supported.

Your emotional intelligence allows you to connect with your child on a deeper level, helping you to understand their thoughts, feelings, and needs. This understanding enables you to respond to their emotions in a way that promotes their emotional well-being and helps them develop healthy coping mechanisms.

As an emotionally intelligent parent, you can model positive emotional regulation and problem-solving skills, teaching your child valuable life lessons that'll serve them well into adulthood.

Importance of emotional intelligence in children's development

Nurturing your child's emotional awareness and understanding their feelings is key in fostering their overall development and well-being. Emotional intelligence plays a crucial role in children's development as it helps them navigate through life's challenges and build healthy relationships.

By teaching children to recognize and manage their emotions, they're better equipped to cope with stress, regulate their behavior, and make positive decisions. Emotional intelligence also promotes empathy and understanding towards others, enhancing their social skills and ability to communicate effectively.

As parents, it's important to create a safe and supportive environment where children feel comfortable expressing their emotions. By validating their feelings and teaching them to label and understand their emotions, we empower them to develop a strong sense of self-awareness and emotional resilience.

Through emotional intelligence, children can develop the necessary skills to thrive in all aspects of their lives, both now and in the future.

Impact of parental emotional intelligence on children

Now that you understand the significance of emotional intelligence in children's development, let's delve into the profound impact that parental emotional intelligence has on their children.

As a parent, your emotional intelligence serves as a powerful model for your child, shaping their understanding and management of their own emotions. When you demonstrate empathy, self-awareness, and effective communication, you teach your child how to navigate their own emotional landscape with confidence and resilience.

By being attuned to your own emotions and expressing them in a healthy way, you provide a safe and supportive environment for your child to explore and express their own feelings. Your emotional intelligence acts as a guide for your child, showing them how to regulate their emotions, solve problems, and build strong relationships.

By nurturing your own emotional intelligence, you empower your child to develop a solid foundation of emotional well-being that will benefit them throughout their lives.

Nurturing Children's Emotional Intelligence

To foster emotional intelligence in your children, it's important to employ strategies that encourage emotional awareness and expression.

This can include creating a safe and supportive environment where your child feels comfortable sharing their feelings, as well as actively listening and validating their emotions.

Additionally, developing their emotional vocabulary through discussions and storytelling can help them better understand and articulate their emotions.

Teaching your child emotional regulation and empathy can also play a crucial role in their emotional intelligence, as it helps them manage their emotions and understand the feelings of others.

Strategies for fostering emotional intelligence in children

Implementing effective strategies for fostering emotional intelligence in children involves creating a supportive environment, encouraging open communication, and modeling healthy emotional expression.

By creating a safe and nurturing environment, children feel more comfortable expressing and exploring their emotions. This can be done by providing a space where they can freely express their feelings without judgment or criticism.

In addition, encouraging open communication allows children to learn how to effectively express their emotions and needs, fostering a sense of empathy and understanding.

By modeling healthy emotional expression, adults can demonstrate to children how to identify and manage their emotions in a positive way. This can include labeling emotions, discussing coping strategies, and practicing self-regulation techniques.

Overall, these strategies help children develop a strong emotional intelligence foundation, enabling them to navigate and understand their emotions effectively.

Developing emotional vocabulary in children

Creating a nurturing environment where children can freely express their feelings helps them develop a rich emotional vocabulary that enables them to better understand and communicate their innermost emotions. By encouraging open and honest dialogue about emotions, parents and caregivers can provide a safe space for children to explore and name their feelings.

This process allows children to become more self-aware and develop a greater understanding of their emotional experiences. As children learn to identify and label their emotions, they are better equipped to express themselves in healthy and constructive ways, which can ultimately lead to improved emotional intelligence.

Additionally, developing an emotional vocabulary empowers children to effectively communicate their needs, desires, and concerns to others, fostering stronger relationships and promoting a sense of empathy and understanding.

Ultimately, by actively engaging in discussions about emotions and providing opportunities for children to articulate their feelings, we can help them develop the necessary skills to navigate their emotions and thrive in their social interactions.

Teaching emotional regulation and empathy to children

Teaching kids how to regulate their emotions and show empathy can be a game-changer in their relationships and overall well-being. When children learn to identify and manage their emotions, they gain a sense of control and are better equipped to handle challenging situations.

By helping them understand that it's normal to feel a wide range of emotions, we empower them to express themselves in a healthy and constructive way. Teaching empathy goes hand in hand with emotional regulation, as it encourages children to consider the feelings and perspectives of others.

By fostering empathy, we are laying the foundation for strong and compassionate relationships, where children learn to value and respect the emotions of those around them. As adults, we play a crucial role in modeling these skills and providing opportunities for children to practice them.

By doing so, we're not only shaping their emotional intelligence but also nurturing their ability to connect with others on a deeper level.

Parental Emotional Intelligence and Parenting Challenges

When it comes to handling conflicts with your children, it's crucial to tap into your parental emotional intelligence. This means being aware of your own emotions and how they impact your reactions and responses.

By developing your emotional intelligence, you can better navigate these conflicts and find constructive solutions that promote healthy communication and understanding.

Additionally, by modeling emotional intelligence in disciplining and setting boundaries, you can teach your children valuable skills in self-regulation and empathy, fostering their emotional growth and resilience.

Parental emotional intelligence in handling conflicts with children

In parenting, mastering the art of conflict resolution with your children requires finesse and a firm grasp on emotional intelligence. It's essential to understand that conflicts are an inevitable part of any parent-child relationship, and how you handle these conflicts can have a long-lasting impact on your child's emotional well-being.

By cultivating your own emotional intelligence, you can effectively navigate through conflicts with your children and teach them valuable skills for managing their emotions. It's important to approach conflicts with empathy and understanding, acknowledging your child's feelings and validating their emotions.

By actively listening to their perspective and engaging in open communication, you can create a safe space for your child to express themselves and find mutually beneficial solutions. Additionally, modeling healthy conflict resolution strategies, such as using 'I'statements and finding compromises, can teach your child valuable skills that they can apply in various aspects of their lives.

Remember, conflict is not a sign of failure in parenting; rather, it's an opportunity for growth and learning for both you and your child.

Emotional intelligence in disciplining and setting boundaries

To effectively discipline and set boundaries with your child, it's crucial for you to understand and empathize with their emotions and needs. By recognizing and acknowledging their feelings, you're showing them that you value their emotions and are willing to listen to them. This not only helps them feel understood but also fosters a sense of trust and connection between you and your child.

It's important to remember that discipline isn't about punishment or control, but rather about teaching and guiding your child towards appropriate behavior. By approaching discipline with empathy, you can help your child develop emotional intelligence and problem-solving skills.

Setting clear boundaries is also essential in teaching your child about limits and acceptable behavior. By setting consistent and reasonable boundaries, you're providing them with a sense of structure and security. However, it's essential to communicate these boundaries in a calm and respectful manner, ensuring that your child understands the reasons behind them.

By practicing emotional intelligence in disciplining and setting boundaries, you're not only helping your child grow and develop but also strengthening your relationship with them.

Modeling emotional intelligence for children

By demonstrating empathy and understanding in your own interactions and relationships, you can effectively model emotional intelligence for your children.

Children learn by observing and imitating the behavior of those around them, so it's crucial to be mindful of how you express and handle emotions.

By showing empathy towards others, you teach your children to understand and validate the feelings of others, fostering their own emotional intelligence.

Additionally, when you demonstrate understanding in your own relationships, you teach your children the importance of open communication and problem-solving skills.

Modeling emotional intelligence not only helps your children develop their own emotional awareness but also creates a positive and supportive environment for them to grow and learn.

Remember, your actions speak louder than words, so make sure to consistently show empathy, understanding, and emotional intelligence in your interactions with others.

X. Emotional Intelligence and Leadership

In this section, we'll delve into the role of emotional intelligence in effective leadership and how to develop emotional intelligence for leadership.

Understanding how emotions impact decision-making, communication, and relationship-building is crucial for leaders to effectively navigate the challenges they face.

Additionally, we'll explore how emotional intelligence influences team dynamics and the importance of fostering emotional intelligence within a team for optimal performance and collaboration.

The Role of Emotional Intelligence in Effective Leadership

When it comes to effective leadership, emotional intelligence plays a crucial role. Understanding and defining emotional intelligence in leadership is essential for guiding and inspiring others.

Emotional intelligence impacts leadership effectiveness by allowing leaders to connect with their teams on a deeper level, empathize with their struggles, and effectively manage conflicts.

Case studies of emotionally intelligent leaders provide real-life examples of how emotional intelligence can drive success and create positive work environments.

By cultivating emotional intelligence, leaders can enhance their ability to lead with empathy, understanding, and authenticity.

Defining emotional intelligence in leadership

Imagine yourself in a leadership role, where your ability to understand and manage emotions, known as emotional intelligence, can greatly influence the success of your team.

Emotional intelligence in leadership refers to the capacity to recognize and regulate your own emotions, as well as understand and empathize with the emotions of others.

It involves being self-aware and able to control your reactions, while also being attuned to the feelings and needs of your team members.

A leader with high emotional intelligence can effectively communicate, build strong relationships, and create a positive and supportive work environment.

By demonstrating empathy, actively listening, and responding appropriately to the emotions of others, you can foster trust and motivation among your team members, leading to improved collaboration and overall success.

Developing emotional intelligence as a leader requires self-reflection, continuous learning, and a genuine desire to connect with and understand others on a deeper level.

It is a skill that can be honed and cultivated over time, and the benefits of emotional intelligence in leadership are invaluable for both the leader and their team.

How emotional intelligence impacts leadership effectiveness

Picture yourself as a leader, where your ability to connect with and understand others on a deeper level can surprisingly enhance your effectiveness.

Emotional intelligence plays a crucial role in leadership as it allows you to effectively navigate the complex dynamics of human relationships. By being aware of and managing your own emotions, you can create a positive and supportive work environment that fosters trust and collaboration.

Additionally, understanding the emotions of others enables you to empathize with their experiences and perspectives, leading to better communication and conflict resolution.

As a leader, having a high emotional intelligence empowers you to inspire and motivate your team, as you're able to recognize and respond to their individual needs and aspirations.

By harnessing the power of emotional intelligence, you can truly unleash your leadership potential and drive sustainable success.

Case studies of emotionally intelligent leaders

Put yourself in the shoes of a leader who effortlessly connects with others and understands them on a deeper level, enhancing your effectiveness in ways you never thought possible. Imagine being able to navigate through complex situations with ease, leveraging your emotional intelligence to inspire and motivate your team.

Case studies of emotionally intelligent leaders have shown that this ability to connect emotionally with others leads to improved communication, stronger relationships, and increased productivity. These leaders possess a keen sense of self-awareness, allowing them to regulate their own emotions and react appropriately to the emotions of those around them. They are able to empathize with their team members, recognizing and validating their feelings, which in turn fosters a sense of trust and loyalty.

Through their ability to understand and manage emotions, emotionally intelligent leaders create a positive work environment where individuals feel valued, supported, and empowered. They are skilled at recognizing and addressing the emotional needs of their team members, leading to higher levels of engagement and job satisfaction. By embodying emotional intelligence, these leaders inspire and motivate their teams to achieve their full potential, ultimately driving organizational success.

Developing Emotional Intelligence for Leadership

To be successful in a leadership role, you need to develop strong emotional intelligence skills. These skills allow you to understand and manage your own emotions, as well as the emotions of others.

Building trust and rapport with your team is essential, as it creates a positive and productive work environment.

Additionally, emotional intelligence plays a crucial role in decision-making and problem-solving, as it allows you to consider the impact of your actions on others and make more informed choices.

Emotional intelligence skills for leadership success

Developing strong emotional intelligence skills is crucial for leaders to achieve success and stand out from the crowd in the dog-eat-dog world of business.

As a leader, you need to be able to understand and manage your own emotions, as well as the emotions of those around you. This means being able to recognize and regulate your own emotions, as well as empathize with and understand the emotions of others.

By developing these skills, you will be better equipped to navigate difficult situations, build strong relationships, and inspire and motivate your team.

Emotional intelligence also allows you to make more informed decisions, as you are able to consider both the rational and emotional aspects of a situation.

In today's fast-paced and competitive business environment, leaders who possess high emotional intelligence are more likely to succeed and make a lasting impact.

So, take the time to invest in developing your emotional intelligence skills and watch as your leadership abilities soar.

Building trust and rapport as a leader

Build trust and rapport with your team by genuinely connecting with them and understanding their needs and concerns.

As a leader, it's essential to create a safe and supportive environment where your team feels comfortable expressing themselves.

Take the time to listen actively and empathetically, showing genuine interest in their thoughts and feelings.

By understanding their needs and concerns, you can address any issues that may arise and provide the necessary support.

Additionally, be transparent and honest in your communication, fostering an atmosphere of trust and reliability.

When your team feels that you genuinely care about their well-being and success, they'll be more motivated and committed to achieving their goals.

Remember, building trust and rapport takes time and effort, but the rewards in terms of team cohesion and productivity are invaluable.

Emotional intelligence in decision-making and problem-solving

Take a moment to reflect on how understanding the emotions of others and effectively solving problems can greatly impact your leadership skills. Emotional intelligence plays a crucial role in decision-making and problem-solving as a leader.

By being attuned to the emotions of those around you, you can better understand their perspectives and motivations, allowing for more informed and empathetic decision-making.

Additionally, emotional intelligence enables you to navigate complex situations with a greater level of sensitivity and understanding, fostering a collaborative and inclusive problem-solving approach.

When you're able to identify and manage your own emotions, you can make rational decisions that aren't clouded by personal biases or external pressures.

Moreover, by considering the emotional impact of your decisions on others, you can build trust and rapport, creating a positive and supportive environment for problem-solving.

Overall, integrating emotional intelligence into your decision-making and problem-solving processes can enhance your leadership effectiveness and contribute to a more cohesive and successful team.

Emotional Intelligence and Team Dynamics

In order to create a positive team culture, it's important to understand the role that emotional intelligence plays.

By being aware of your own emotions and those of your team members, you can better navigate the dynamics of the group and foster a supportive and collaborative environment.

Effective communication and collaboration also rely heavily on emotional intelligence, as it allows you to understand and empathize with others' perspectives and needs.

Lastly, emotional intelligence is crucial in conflict resolution and team motivation. It enables you to handle disagreements and challenges with empathy and understanding, while also motivating and inspiring your team to achieve their goals.

Emotional intelligence in creating a positive team culture

Fostering emotional intelligence can be the key to cultivating a vibrant and harmonious team culture. When team members are emotionally intelligent, they're able to understand and manage their own emotions as well as empathize with others.

This creates an environment where individuals feel valued, heard, and supported, leading to increased trust and collaboration. Emotional intelligence also promotes effective communication, as team members are better able to express their thoughts and feelings in a constructive and respectful manner.

By prioritizing emotional intelligence in team dynamics, leaders can create a positive and inclusive culture that encourages open dialogue, creativity, and innovation. This ultimately leads to higher levels of engagement, productivity, and overall team success.

Emotional intelligence for effective communication and collaboration

Developing strong emotional intelligence skills enables you to effectively communicate and collaborate with your team members. According to a study conducted by Harvard Business Review, teams with high emotional intelligence experienced a 12% increase in project success rates.

By understanding and managing your own emotions, you can better express yourself and connect with others. This allows for clearer and more effective communication, leading to better collaboration and problem-solving.

Additionally, emotional intelligence helps you to be more empathetic and understanding towards your colleagues, creating a positive and supportive team environment. By cultivating emotional intelligence, you can build stronger relationships, enhance team dynamics, and ultimately achieve greater success in your projects.

Emotional intelligence in conflict resolution and team motivation

By effectively managing and understanding our own emotions, we can navigate conflicts and motivate our team members to achieve success. Conflict resolution requires emotional intelligence because it involves understanding and empathizing with the perspectives and emotions of others involved.

By recognizing and acknowledging our own emotions in a conflict, we can respond in a more rational and controlled manner, leading to more productive discussions and resolutions. Additionally, emotional intelligence plays a crucial role in motivating our team members.

By understanding their individual emotions and needs, we can provide the necessary support and encouragement to help them overcome obstacles and achieve their goals. Empathy and effective communication are key in this process, as they allow us to connect with others on a deeper level and create a positive and motivating work environment.

Ultimately, by harnessing emotional intelligence in conflict resolution and team motivation, we can foster stronger relationships, increase productivity, and drive overall success.

XI. Emotional Intelligence in Conflict Resolution

In understanding conflict and emotional intelligence, it's important to recognize the role emotions play in conflict resolution.

Emotional intelligence can help individuals navigate conflicts by understanding their own emotions and those of others involved.

By employing strategies such as active listening, empathy, and effective communication, emotional intelligence can foster a more constructive and empathetic approach to conflict resolution.

Understanding Conflict and Emotional Intelligence

When it comes to understanding conflict and its emotional aspects, it's important to define what conflict means and how it affects us emotionally.

Conflict is not just a disagreement or a clash of opinions, but it also triggers a range of emotions such as anger, frustration, and hurt.

Emotional intelligence plays a crucial role in resolving conflicts as it helps us understand and manage our own emotions, as well as the emotions of others involved.

By developing emotional intelligence skills such as empathy, active listening, and effective communication, you can navigate conflicts peacefully and find mutually beneficial resolutions.

Defining conflict and its emotional aspects

Conflict is an intricate dance of emotions that can reveal hidden aspects of your emotional intelligence. It is a complex interplay of thoughts, feelings, and behaviors that arise when there's a perceived disagreement or clash of interests between individuals or groups.

In the heat of conflict, emotions can run high, and it's often difficult to separate the rational from the irrational. However, conflict also provides an opportunity for growth and self-reflection. By understanding the emotional aspects of conflict, you can gain insight into your own triggers and patterns of behavior, as well as develop the ability to empathize with others and effectively manage your emotions.

Conflict challenges you to navigate through a myriad of emotions such as anger, frustration, fear, and sadness. It's through this process that you can deepen your emotional intelligence and build stronger relationships.

The role of emotional intelligence in conflict resolution

The art of navigating through the intricate dance of emotions in conflict resolution involves tapping into your emotional finesse and understanding the subtle nuances of human interaction.

Emotional intelligence plays a crucial role in resolving conflicts as it allows you to effectively manage your own emotions and empathize with others.

By being aware of your own emotions and the emotions of others, you can better navigate the complexities of conflict and find common ground.

Emotional intelligence helps you recognize when emotions may be escalating and allows you to respond in a calm and rational manner.

It also enables you to understand the underlying issues and needs of all parties involved, fostering a sense of empathy and creating a safe space for open communication.

By utilizing emotional intelligence, you can enhance your ability to resolve conflicts and build stronger and more meaningful relationships.

Emotional intelligence skills for resolving conflicts peacefully

Use your keen understanding of people's feelings and your ability to connect with them to peacefully resolve conflicts.

Emotional intelligence skills play a crucial role in conflict resolution as they enable you to navigate through tense situations with empathy and insight.

By actively listening and validating the emotions of others, you can create a safe space for open communication, fostering a deeper understanding of each other's perspectives.

Additionally, being aware of your own emotions and managing them effectively allows you to remain calm and composed during conflicts, preventing escalation.

Through emotional intelligence, you can identify common ground, find mutually beneficial solutions, and build stronger relationships based on trust and respect.

Remember, resolving conflicts peacefully requires not only addressing the surface-level issues but also addressing the underlying emotions and needs of all parties involved.

Emotional Intelligence Strategies for Conflict Resolution

In order to effectively navigate conflicts, it's important to employ emotional intelligence strategies.

By actively listening and showing empathy, you can create a safe space for open communication and understanding between parties.

Additionally, emotional self-regulation is crucial for managing conflicts in a productive manner. It allows you to respond rather than react impulsively.

Lastly, by utilizing emotional intelligence, you can strive to find win-win solutions. These solutions take into consideration both parties' needs and interests, leading to a more harmonious resolution.

Active listening and empathy in conflict resolution

Engaging in active listening and practicing empathy is like lighting a path through the darkness of conflict resolution. When you truly listen to the other person, not just hearing their words but understanding their emotions and perspective, you create a safe space for open communication.

By actively engaging in the conversation, asking clarifying questions, and reflecting back what you hear, you show the other person that you value their thoughts and feelings. This allows them to feel heard and validated, which can help diffuse tension and create a foundation for finding common ground.

Additionally, empathy plays a crucial role in conflict resolution. When you put yourself in the other person's shoes and try to understand their emotions and motivations, you can develop a deeper sense of empathy and compassion. This can lead to a more understanding and collaborative approach to resolving the conflict, as you are able to acknowledge and address the underlying emotions driving the disagreement.

By combining active listening and empathy, you can navigate the complexities of conflict resolution with greater ease and effectiveness.

Emotional self-regulation for effective conflict management

Practicing emotional self-regulation is key to effectively managing conflicts. When faced with conflict, it's natural to feel a surge of emotions, such as anger, frustration, or sadness. However, allowing these emotions to dictate our actions can often lead to further escalation and damage in relationships.

By learning to regulate and control our emotions, we can approach conflicts with a clear and rational mindset. This allows us to communicate our needs and concerns in a calm and assertive manner, fostering a more productive and empathetic dialogue. Emotional self-regulation also enables us to actively listen to the other party's perspective, understanding their emotions and experiences without getting overwhelmed by our own.

It allows us to respond rather than react, making space for empathy and finding mutually beneficial solutions. So, the next time you find yourself in a conflict, take a moment to pause, breathe, and regulate your emotions before responding. This simple practice can make a significant difference in resolving conflicts effectively and maintaining healthy relationships.

Finding win-win solutions through emotional intelligence

Utilizing emotional self-awareness and regulating your own responses, you can effectively navigate conflicts and find mutually beneficial solutions.

By understanding your own emotions and triggers, you can approach conflict with a sense of calmness and clarity. This allows you to listen actively to the other person's perspective and truly understand their needs and concerns.

With emotional intelligence, you can empathize with their emotions and validate their experiences, creating a sense of trust and openness. By finding common ground and exploring creative solutions, you can work together to find win-win outcomes that satisfy both parties' interests.

Emotional intelligence enables you to communicate effectively, manage your emotions, and build strong relationships, fostering collaboration and cooperation in conflict resolution. With these skills, you can transform conflicts into opportunities for growth and create harmonious and productive relationships.

XII. Emotional Intelligence in Communication

In this subtopic, you'll explore the importance of emotional intelligence in communication. By understanding and managing your own emotions, you can enhance your communication skills and build stronger connections with others.

Additionally, you'll learn how emotional intelligence can be particularly useful in challenging communication situations, helping you navigate conflicts and effectively express yourself.

The Importance of Emotional Intelligence in Communication

Understanding the impact of emotional intelligence on effective communication is crucial. When you possess emotional intelligence skills, you're better equipped to communicate clearly and empathetically.

This allows you to connect with others on a deeper level, fostering understanding and building strong relationships.

The benefits of emotionally intelligent communication are numerous, as it leads to improved collaboration, conflict resolution, and overall positive interactions.

Understanding the impact of emotional intelligence on effective communication

Mastering emotional intelligence is crucial for effective communication, allowing you to connect deeply with others and convey your message with impact.

Understanding the impact of emotional intelligence on communication means recognizing that emotions play a significant role in how we interpret and respond to messages.

By developing your emotional intelligence, you can better understand and manage your own emotions, which in turn allows you to respond to others in a more empathetic and effective manner.

This heightened self-awareness allows you to be more attuned to the emotions of others, enabling you to tailor your communication style to meet their needs.

Additionally, emotional intelligence helps you navigate conflicts and difficult conversations with grace and understanding, fostering stronger relationships and promoting mutual understanding.

By honing your emotional intelligence, you can become a more effective communicator, building deeper connections and achieving greater success in your personal and professional relationships.

Emotional intelligence skills for clear and empathetic communication

Developing strong emotional awareness and empathy allows you to effectively connect with others and convey your message with impact, resulting in clear and compassionate communication. By honing your emotional intelligence skills, you can understand and manage your own emotions, as well as recognize and empathize with the emotions of others.

This heightened self-awareness and empathy enable you to communicate in a way that resonates with people on a deeper level, fostering trust and understanding. When you're aware of your emotions, you can express yourself authentically and assertively, while also considering the feelings and perspectives of others. This leads to more open and honest conversations, where both parties feel heard and validated.

Additionally, emotional intelligence allows you to navigate difficult conversations with empathy and compassion, allowing for a more peaceful resolution and stronger relationships. By investing in your emotional intelligence skills, you can become a master communicator, capable of creating meaningful connections and fostering a positive and inclusive environment.

Benefits of emotionally intelligent communication

By harnessing the power of emotional awareness and empathy, you can experience a whole new level of connection and understanding in your interactions, leading to more fulfilling and harmonious relationships.

When you communicate with emotional intelligence, you're able to truly understand and empathize with others, creating a safe and supportive space for open and honest communication. This level of communication allows you to address conflicts and misunderstandings in a productive and respectful manner, leading to greater resolution and deeper connections.

Additionally, emotionally intelligent communication fosters trust and strengthens relationships, as it shows that you genuinely care about others' feelings and perspectives. It allows you to validate and acknowledge their emotions, which can help to create a sense of belonging and acceptance.

Ultimately, emotionally intelligent communication not only enhances your relationships but also promotes personal growth and self-awareness. It enables you to better understand your own emotions and reactions, leading to improved self-regulation and a greater sense of emotional well-being.

Enhancing Communication Skills through Emotional Intelligence

In this discussion, we'll explore how emotional intelligence can enhance your communication skills.

One key aspect is active listening and empathetic responding, where you truly engage with others and respond in a way that shows understanding and compassion.

Additionally, we'll delve into the role of non-verbal communication and emotional intelligence, as our body language and facial expressions can convey a wealth of emotions.

Lastly, we'll examine the connection between assertiveness and emotional intelligence in communication, as being assertive while still considering the emotions of others is crucial for effective interactions.

By developing your emotional intelligence, you can become a more skilled and empathetic communicator.

Active listening and empathetic responding

Active listening and empathetic responding are essential skills for effective communication. When you actively listen to someone, you're fully present in the conversation, giving them your undivided attention. This means not only hearing their words but also paying attention to their body language, tone of voice, and emotions.

By doing so, you can truly understand their perspective and validate their feelings. Empathetic responding goes hand in hand with active listening, as it involves acknowledging and expressing understanding of the other person's emotions. When you respond empathetically, you create a safe space for them to share their thoughts and feelings without fear of judgment.

This not only strengthens the connection between you and the other person but also fosters trust and mutual respect. By actively listening and responding empathetically, you can enhance your communication skills and build deeper, more meaningful relationships.

Non-verbal communication and emotional intelligence

Non-verbal cues, such as facial expressions and gestures, play a crucial role in understanding and connecting with others on a deeper level. When you observe someone's facial expressions, you can gain valuable insights into their emotions and feelings.

A smile can indicate happiness and warmth, while a furrowed brow may suggest worry or concern. Similarly, gestures like nodding or leaning in can signal attentiveness and interest.

By paying attention to these non-verbal cues, you can better understand the emotional state of others and respond in a way that shows empathy and support. It allows you to go beyond just listening to someone's words and truly connect with them on an emotional level.

So, next time you engage in a conversation, remember to be mindful of the non-verbal cues that can provide you with valuable information about the other person's emotional well-being.

Assertiveness and emotional intelligence in communication

Assertiveness and emotional intelligence are key aspects of effective communication. When you communicate assertively, you're able to express your thoughts and feelings in a clear and direct manner, without being aggressive or passive. This allows you to assert your needs and boundaries while also considering the feelings and perspectives of others.

Assertiveness shows that you value yourself and your opinions, and it encourages open and honest communication. When combined with emotional intelligence, assertiveness becomes even more powerful. Emotional intelligence is the ability to recognize, understand, and manage your own emotions, as well as the emotions of others.

It allows you to empathize with others, listen actively, and respond appropriately to different situations. By being assertive and emotionally intelligent in your communication, you can build strong and meaningful relationships, resolve conflicts effectively, and create a positive and supportive environment for everyone involved.

Emotional Intelligence in Challenging Communication Situations

When it comes to communicating with difficult people, emotional intelligence can be a powerful tool. By using emotional intelligence, you can navigate challenging conversations with grace and empathy, allowing for more productive and positive outcomes.

Conflict resolution conversations can also benefit greatly from emotional intelligence, as it helps you understand the emotions and perspectives of all parties involved, leading to more effective and mutually satisfying resolutions.

Additionally, emotional intelligence can help you overcome barriers to effective communication, such as misunderstandings, defensiveness, and lack of trust, by promoting understanding, active listening, and open dialogue.

Communicating with difficult people through emotional

intelligence

Dealing with challenging individuals requires you to tap into your emotional intelligence, allowing you to navigate the stormy seas of communication with finesse and grace.

It's crucial to approach these interactions with a sense of empathy and understanding, recognizing that difficult people may be driven by their own unresolved emotions or insecurities.

By actively listening and validating their feelings, you can create a safe space for them to express themselves without feeling judged or attacked.

It's also important to remain calm and composed, as reacting impulsively or defensively may only escalate the situation further.

Instead, try to identify the underlying emotions behind their behavior and respond in a way that addresses those emotions.

By practicing emotional intelligence, you can effectively communicate with difficult people, fostering understanding and building stronger relationships.

Emotional intelligence in conflict resolution conversations

Mastering the art of effective communication during conflict resolution conversations involves understanding the emotions and perspectives of others, allowing you to find common ground and work towards a mutually beneficial solution.

When engaging in these conversations, it's crucial to approach the situation with empathy and insight. By actively listening to the other person's concerns and emotions, you can better understand their point of view and validate their feelings. This validation creates a sense of trust and openness, which can lead to a more productive dialogue.

Additionally, it's important to express your own emotions and perspectives in a clear and respectful manner. By doing so, you can foster understanding and create an environment where both parties feel heard and valued.

Conflict resolution conversations require emotional intelligence, as it allows you to navigate through challenging emotions and find resolutions that address the underlying issues. By employing these skills, you can foster healthier relationships and build stronger connections with others.

Overcoming barriers to effective communication with emotional intelligence

To effectively navigate through communication barriers, imagine yourself as a skilled communicator effortlessly connecting with others, creating a harmonious and open space for understanding and resolving conflicts.

By employing emotional intelligence, you can overcome these barriers and enhance your communication skills. One of the key aspects of emotional intelligence is self-awareness, which allows you to understand your own emotions and how they may impact your communication. By being aware of your emotions, you can regulate them and prevent them from interfering with effective communication.

Additionally, empathetic listening is crucial in overcoming communication barriers. By truly listening and understanding the perspectives and emotions of others, you can create a safe and open environment for communication.

Finally, effective communication requires clarity in expressing your thoughts and emotions. By using clear and concise language, you can ensure that your message is understood and avoid any misinterpretations.

By incorporating emotional intelligence into your communication, you can break down barriers and foster understanding and resolution in your interactions with others.

XIII. Emotional Intelligence and Personal Growth

When it comes to personal growth, emotional intelligence plays a crucial role in your journey.

Cultivating emotional intelligence can lead to personal transformation, as it allows you to understand and manage your emotions effectively.

By developing your emotional intelligence, you can also find fulfillment in both your personal and professional life, as it enables you to build stronger relationships and make more informed decisions.

Personal Growth and Emotional Intelligence

Emotional intelligence can serve as a powerful catalyst for your personal growth. By recognizing and understanding your own emotions, you'll be better equipped to navigate through life's challenges and make thoughtful decisions.

Through self-reflection and self-analysis, you can actively work on developing your emotional intelligence. This will allow you to build stronger relationships and enhance your overall well-being.

By setting goals for personal growth with emotional intelligence in mind, you can create a roadmap for success and fulfillment. This ensures that your actions align with your values and aspirations.

Emotional intelligence as a catalyst for personal growth

Developing emotional intelligence is like unlocking the hidden power within yourself, propelling your personal growth to new heights. By understanding and managing your emotions, you gain a deeper understanding of yourself and others. This allows you to navigate relationships and challenges with greater ease.

Emotional intelligence acts as a catalyst for personal growth because it helps you become more self-aware. This enables you to identify and address any underlying emotional issues that may be holding you back. It also enhances your ability to empathize with others, fostering stronger connections and improving your communication skills.

As you develop emotional intelligence, you become more resilient in the face of adversity. You are better equipped to handle stress and more adept at making decisions that align with your values and goals.

Ultimately, emotional intelligence empowers you to lead a more fulfilling and purposeful life. It enables you to not only understand yourself better but also to positively impact the world around you.

Self-reflection and self-analysis for personal development

Now that you understand the significance of emotional intelligence as a catalyst for personal growth, it's time to delve deeper into the tools that can help you develop this crucial skill.

Self-reflection and self-analysis are essential components of personal development, allowing you to gain a deeper understanding of your emotions, thoughts, and behaviors. By taking the time to pause and reflect on your experiences, you can uncover patterns, triggers, and underlying beliefs that may be holding you back from reaching your full potential.

Self-analysis involves being honest with yourself, asking probing questions, and examining your actions and reactions. This process can be both enlightening and challenging, as it requires you to confront uncomfortable truths and face your vulnerabilities. However, by embracing this journey of self-discovery, you can gain valuable insights, identify areas for improvement, and ultimately pave the way for personal growth and emotional intelligence.

Setting goals for personal growth with emotional intelligence

Take a step forward on your journey towards personal growth by envisioning your future self as a blooming flower, ready to blossom and thrive with the guidance of emotional intelligence.

Setting goals for personal growth with emotional intelligence is a powerful tool that allows you to tap into your innermost desires and aspirations. It helps you identify areas of improvement, understand your strengths and weaknesses, and create a roadmap to achieve your full potential.

By setting clear and realistic goals, you are actively engaging in self-reflection and self-analysis, which are essential for personal development. Emotional intelligence empowers you to recognize and manage your emotions, enabling you to navigate through challenges and setbacks with resilience and adaptability. It provides you with the skills to build meaningful relationships, understand the needs and perspectives of others, and communicate effectively.

As you embark on this journey, remember to be kind and patient with yourself. Growth takes time, effort, and dedication. Celebrate each milestone along the way and embrace the lessons learned from setbacks.

With emotional intelligence as your guide, you have the power to transform into the best version of yourself, blooming and thriving in all aspects of life.

Cultivating Emotional Intelligence for Personal Transformation

In this discussion, we'll explore how cultivating emotional intelligence can lead to personal transformation in various aspects of your life.

One key point to consider is the relationship between emotional intelligence and self-confidence. By understanding and managing your emotions effectively, you can develop a strong sense of self-assurance and belief in your abilities.

Additionally, we'll examine how emotional intelligence can help you overcome limiting beliefs that may be holding you back from reaching your full potential.

Lastly, we'll discuss the importance of developing emotional intelligence during times of change and transition. It can provide you with the tools and resilience needed to navigate these challenges successfully.

Emotional intelligence and self-confidence

Improve your emotional intelligence and boost your self-confidence with the techniques explained in 'The Emotion Code.'

By understanding and decoding your emotions, you can gain a deeper insight into yourself and others, leading to more meaningful connections and personal growth. Developing emotional intelligence allows you to navigate challenging situations with grace and empathy, as you become more attuned to your own emotions and the emotions of those around you.

As you cultivate this skill, you'll notice a positive shift in your self-confidence, as you gain a better understanding of your strengths and weaknesses. The Emotion Code provides practical tools and exercises to help you develop emotional intelligence, enabling you to build strong relationships, make informed decisions, and thrive in both personal and professional settings.

So why not embark on this transformative journey and unlock the power of emotional intelligence to enhance your self-confidence and overall well-being?

Overcoming limiting beliefs through emotional intelligence

Challenge your beliefs and open yourself up to new possibilities by developing a deeper understanding of your emotions and the impact they have on your perspective and decision-making.

Often, we're held back by limiting beliefs that prevent us from reaching our full potential. These beliefs are shaped by past experiences, societal norms, and our own self-doubt.

However, through emotional intelligence, we can identify and overcome these limiting beliefs. By recognizing our emotions and the thoughts that accompany them, we can begin to question the validity of our beliefs. Are they based on facts or are they simply assumptions we've made?

Emotional intelligence allows us to challenge these beliefs and explore alternative perspectives. It helps us see that our emotions aren't always an accurate reflection of reality and that we have the power to change our mindset.

By developing emotional intelligence, we can break free from the constraints of limiting beliefs and open ourselves up to new opportunities and experiences. It takes courage and self-reflection, but the rewards are worth it.

So, take the leap and start exploring the power of emotional intelligence in overcoming your limiting beliefs.

Developing emotional intelligence in times of change and transition

Navigating through periods of change and transition can be a transformative journey when you cultivate a deeper understanding of your own emotions and their impact.

It is during these times that emotions can run high, and it can be easy to feel overwhelmed or lost.

However, by developing emotional intelligence, you can navigate through these challenges with greater ease and clarity.

Emotional intelligence allows you to not only recognize and acknowledge your own emotions, but also understand how they may be influencing your thoughts and behaviors.

This self-awareness is crucial in times of change, as it enables you to make conscious choices and respond in a way that aligns with your values and goals.

Additionally, emotional intelligence helps you navigate the emotions of others, allowing you to build stronger relationships and communicate effectively during times of uncertainty.

By developing emotional intelligence, you are equipping yourself with a powerful tool that can support you in embracing change, adapting to new circumstances, and ultimately, thriving in times of transition.

Emotional Intelligence and Finding Fulfillment

When it comes to finding fulfillment in life, aligning your values and purpose with emotional intelligence can be a game-changer.

By understanding and managing your own emotions, you can make better choices that are in line with what truly matters to you.

Additionally, emotional intelligence can greatly enhance your relationships, allowing you to connect on a deeper level and find fulfillment through meaningful connections.

Lastly, emotional intelligence plays a vital role in self-actualization, as it allows you to tap into your full potential and live a life that is authentic and true to yourself.

Aligning values and purpose with emotional intelligence

In order to truly align our values and purpose with emotional intelligence, you must be willing to dig deep and uncover the hidden gems within yourself. It requires a level of self-awareness and introspection that may be uncomfortable at times, but the rewards are worth it.

By exploring your core values and understanding what truly matters to you, you can begin to make decisions and take actions that are in alignment with your authentic self. This process also involves examining your purpose - what drives you, what brings you fulfillment, and what impact you want to make in the world.

Emotional intelligence allows you to tap into your emotions and use them as a guide to navigate through life, making choices that are congruent with your values and purpose. It requires empathy, both for yourself and others, as you recognize and acknowledge your emotions and the emotions of those around you.

By aligning your values and purpose with emotional intelligence, you can lead a more fulfilling and meaningful life, where your actions are guided by your authentic self and contribute to your overall well-being and happiness.

Finding fulfillment in relationships through emotional intelligence

Discovering fulfillment in your relationships is possible through the cultivation of a deep understanding and connection with the emotions and needs of both yourself and others. By developing emotional intelligence, you can navigate the complexities of human interactions with empathy and insight.

It starts with recognizing and acknowledging your own emotions, as well as understanding the underlying causes behind them. This self-awareness allows you to communicate your needs and boundaries effectively, fostering healthier and more authentic connections.

Additionally, emotional intelligence enables you to empathize with others, recognizing their emotions and responding with compassion. It involves active listening, validating their feelings, and offering support when needed.

By prioritizing emotional intelligence in your relationships, you create an environment of trust, understanding, and mutual respect. This fosters a deep sense of fulfillment as you forge meaningful connections and experience the joy of truly being seen and understood by others.

Emotional intelligence and self-actualization

Now that you've gained a deeper understanding of how emotional intelligence can enhance your relationships, let's delve into the powerful connection between emotional intelligence and self-actualization.

Self-actualization, a concept introduced by Abraham Maslow, refers to the realization of one's full potential and the pursuit of personal growth and fulfillment.

Emotional intelligence plays a crucial role in this process as it enables you to better understand and manage your own emotions, paving the way for self-awareness and self-acceptance.

By honing your emotional intelligence skills, you can navigate the complexities of your inner world, identify and overcome limiting beliefs, and cultivate a sense of purpose and authenticity in your life.

Through this journey of self-discovery and self-actualization, emotional intelligence becomes an invaluable tool that empowers you to live a more meaningful and fulfilling existence.

XIV. Emotional Intelligence and Cultural Competence

In this discussion, you'll explore the important connection between cultural competence and emotional intelligence. By understanding and developing your emotional intelligence, you can enhance your ability to navigate and adapt to diverse cultural contexts.

Furthermore, you'll examine how emotional intelligence plays a crucial role in fostering meaningful and harmonious intercultural relationships.

Cultural Competence and Emotional Intelligence

Understanding cultural competence and its relationship with emotional intelligence is crucial in today's diverse world.

Culturally competent emotional intelligence allows you to effectively understand, navigate, and connect with individuals from different cultures.

By embracing cultural competence and emotional intelligence, you can reap the benefits of enhanced communication, empathy, and collaboration in multicultural settings.

Emotional intelligence plays a vital role in successfully navigating diverse cultural contexts by enabling you to recognize and manage your own emotions, understand others' perspectives, and adapt your behavior to different cultural norms.

Understanding cultural competence and its relationship with emotional intelligence

Cultural competence is like a key that unlocks the door to emotional intelligence, allowing you to navigate diverse cultural landscapes with ease. It's the ability to recognize, understand, and appreciate different cultures, and the skills to effectively interact with people from various backgrounds.

When you're culturally competent, you possess the knowledge and awareness of cultural norms, values, and beliefs. This helps you to better understand the emotions, experiences, and perspectives of others. This understanding and empathy are crucial components of emotional intelligence, as they enable you to build meaningful connections, communicate effectively, and resolve conflicts in a culturally sensitive manner.

By embracing cultural competence, you not only enhance your emotional intelligence but also foster inclusivity, respect, and harmony in your relationships and interactions with people from different cultures.

Benefits of culturally competent emotional intelligence

Now that you have a better understanding of cultural competence and its relationship with emotional intelligence, let's explore the benefits of having culturally competent emotional intelligence.

Culturally competent emotional intelligence allows you to navigate diverse social and cultural environments with ease and sensitivity. By recognizing and understanding the emotions and experiences of individuals from different cultural backgrounds, you can establish meaningful connections and build strong relationships.

Culturally competent emotional intelligence also enables you to effectively communicate and collaborate with people from diverse backgrounds, fostering inclusivity and respect. Moreover, it helps you to challenge stereotypes and biases, promoting a more inclusive and understanding society.

Ultimately, having culturally competent emotional intelligence not only enhances your personal growth but also contributes to creating a more harmonious and empathetic world.

The role of emotional intelligence in navigating diverse cultural contexts

Explore how your ability to navigate diverse cultural contexts is enhanced by your emotional intelligence. Understanding and managing your own emotions allows you to approach interactions with individuals from different cultures with empathy and sensitivity.

By being aware of your own biases and emotions, you can better navigate challenging situations and adapt your communication style to be more culturally sensitive.

Emotional intelligence also helps you recognize and understand the emotions of others, allowing you to connect on a deeper level and build meaningful relationships across cultural barriers.

With emotional intelligence, you can effectively navigate cultural nuances, adapt to different communication styles, and foster a sense of inclusion and understanding in diverse cultural contexts.

Developing Cultural Competence through Emotional Intelligence

In order to develop cultural competence through emotional intelligence, it's crucial to cultivate empathy and tolerance for cultural differences. By understanding and appreciating the unique perspectives and values of different cultures, you can create a more inclusive and accepting environment.

Additionally, emotional intelligence can help you recognize and challenge your own personal biases, allowing for personal growth and a deeper understanding of others.

Finally, by enhancing communication and relationship-building skills across cultures, you can foster connections and bridge gaps, creating a more harmonious and unified community.

Cultivating empathy and tolerance for cultural differences

Developing empathy and tolerance for cultural differences is like opening a door to a world of colorful tapestries, where you can appreciate the beauty and uniqueness of each thread. It allows you to step outside of your own experiences and perspectives, and truly understand and connect with people from diverse backgrounds.

By cultivating empathy, you develop the ability to put yourself in someone else's shoes, to feel what they feel, and to see the world through their eyes. This not only enhances your emotional intelligence but also fosters a deeper understanding and appreciation for cultural diversity.

Tolerance, on the other hand, involves accepting and respecting differences without judgment or prejudice. It means recognizing that each culture has its own values, beliefs, and practices, and that these differences should be embraced rather than feared.

When you combine empathy and tolerance, you create a space where cultural exchange can thrive, where individuals can learn from one another, and where stereotypes and biases can be challenged and dismantled.

This journey of developing empathy and tolerance is not always easy, as it requires self-reflection, open-mindedness, and a willingness to step outside of your comfort zone. However, the rewards are immeasurable, as it allows us to build bridges of understanding, foster inclusivity, and create a more harmonious and interconnected world.

Recognizing and challenging personal biases through emotional intelligence

Take a moment to reflect on your own biases and how they may be influencing your perceptions and interactions with others.

It's natural for each of us to have biases, shaped by our experiences, upbringing, and societal influences. However, it is crucial to recognize that these biases can hinder our ability to truly understand and connect with others.

Emotional intelligence allows us to challenge these biases by cultivating self-awareness and empathy. By acknowledging our biases, we can actively work towards breaking down the barriers they create and fostering a more inclusive and compassionate environment.

This requires a willingness to listen and learn from diverse perspectives, to question our assumptions, and to challenge the stereotypes we may hold.

It is through this process that we can truly embrace the beauty of diversity and cultivate genuine connections with others.

Enhancing communication and relationship-building across cultures

Improve your cross-cultural communication and relationship-building skills by embracing diversity and actively seeking to understand and appreciate different cultural perspectives.

For example, imagine you're working on a team with members from various cultural backgrounds. By taking the time to learn about their customs, values, and communication styles, you can foster a more inclusive and collaborative environment where everyone feels valued and understood.

Developing cultural intelligence allows you to navigate potential misunderstandings and conflicts by recognizing and respecting the differences in cultural norms. It also enables you to adapt your communication style and approach to build trust and rapport with individuals from different cultures.

By embracing diversity and actively seeking to understand and appreciate different cultural perspectives, you can enhance your cross-cultural communication and relationship-building skills, creating a more harmonious and productive environment for all involved.

Emotional Intelligence and Intercultural Relationships

In cross-cultural partnerships and friendships, emotional intelligence plays a crucial role in understanding and navigating the complexities of different cultural backgrounds. It involves being aware of and empathizing with the emotions of others, as well as effectively expressing one's own emotions.

In multicultural work settings, emotional intelligence becomes even more important as it allows individuals to work collaboratively, respect diversity, and overcome cultural barriers. By developing emotional intelligence, individuals can bridge cultural gaps, foster understanding, and build meaningful connections with people from different backgrounds.

Emotional intelligence in cross-cultural partnerships and

friendships

Explore the depths of emotional intelligence in your cross-cultural partnerships and friendships, understanding that it's the key to building strong connections and fostering mutual understanding.

When engaging in relationships with individuals from different cultural backgrounds, emotional intelligence plays a crucial role in navigating the complexities and potential misunderstandings that may arise.

It requires a deep level of self-awareness, empathy, and an ability to recognize and manage one's own emotions, as well as understand and respond to the emotions of others.

By honing your emotional intelligence, you can develop the skills necessary to communicate effectively, adapt to different cultural norms, and build trust and rapport with your cross-cultural partners and friends.

This will enable you to bridge the gaps and overcome any barriers that may exist, promoting a sense of unity and harmony in your relationships.

Emotional intelligence in multicultural work settings

Thriving in multicultural work settings requires you to possess a deep understanding and awareness of the diverse emotional landscape that exists within the team.

In these settings, you'll encounter colleagues from different cultural backgrounds, each with their own unique set of emotions, communication styles, and ways of expressing themselves.

It's crucial to be empathetic and sensitive to these differences, as it can greatly impact the dynamics and productivity of the team.

By actively developing your emotional intelligence, you can navigate and bridge these cultural gaps, fostering open communication, trust, and collaboration.

This involves being attentive to non-verbal cues, actively listening, and adapting your communication style to meet the needs of your colleagues.

Embracing diversity and cultivating emotional intelligence in multicultural work settings not only enhances team performance but also promotes a more inclusive and harmonious work environment.

Bridging cultural gaps through emotional intelligence

By developing a deep understanding of the diverse emotional landscape in multicultural work settings, you can bridge cultural gaps and foster a more inclusive and harmonious environment.

When you take the time to truly comprehend the emotions and perspectives of individuals from different cultural backgrounds, you open the door to effective communication and collaboration.

Emotional intelligence allows you to empathize with others, recognizing and validating their emotions, regardless of cultural differences. This level of understanding helps to build trust and connection, creating a safe space where individuals feel valued and heard.

By embracing emotional intelligence, you can break down barriers, promote respect, and cultivate a work culture that celebrates diversity.

Through empathy and a willingness to learn from one another, you have the power to bridge cultural gaps and create an environment where everyone can thrive.

XV. Emotional Intelligence and Mindfulness

In this discussion, we'll explore the intersection of emotional intelligence and mindfulness and how these two concepts can complement each other in our daily lives. By combining emotional intelligence and mindfulness practices, we can develop a deeper understanding of our emotions and how they impact our thoughts and behaviors.

Additionally, mindful living can enhance our emotional intelligence by helping us stay present, non-judgmental, and compassionate towards ourselves and others.

The Intersection of Emotional Intelligence and Mindfulness

When it comes to understanding emotional intelligence and mindfulness, it's important to recognize the strong intersection between the two. By incorporating mindfulness practices into the development of emotional intelligence, individuals can reap numerous benefits.

Mindfulness serves as a powerful tool for fostering emotional self-awareness and regulation. It allows individuals to navigate their emotions more effectively.

Understanding the relationship between emotional intelligence and mindfulness

Practicing mindfulness takes emotional intelligence to a whole new level, transporting you to a serene state of self-awareness and enlightenment.

When you engage in mindfulness, you're actively observing your thoughts, feelings, and sensations without judgment. This act of nonjudgmental awareness requires emotional intelligence because it involves recognizing and accepting your emotions as they arise in the present moment.

By cultivating emotional intelligence, you develop the ability to understand and regulate your emotions effectively, which in turn enhances your mindfulness practice.

As you become more emotionally intelligent, you become better equipped to identify and navigate your emotional landscape, allowing for a deeper level of self-awareness and insight.

Furthermore, emotional intelligence enables you to approach your mindfulness practice with empathy, compassion, and kindness towards yourself and others.

By combining emotional intelligence and mindfulness, you can tap into a state of inner peace and clarity, fostering personal growth and well-being.

Benefits of incorporating mindfulness practices into emotional intelligence development

Explore the numerous advantages of integrating mindfulness practices into your journey of developing emotional intelligence. By incorporating mindfulness into your daily routine, you can cultivate a heightened sense of self-awareness and emotional regulation.

Mindfulness allows you to observe your thoughts and emotions without judgment, helping you understand the root causes of your emotional reactions. This increased awareness empowers you to make conscious choices about how you respond to challenging situations, rather than reacting impulsively.

Additionally, mindfulness practices can enhance your ability to empathize with others and improve your interpersonal relationships. By being fully present in the moment, you can actively listen and connect with others on a deeper level, fostering understanding and compassion.

Moreover, mindfulness can reduce stress and anxiety, promoting overall well-being. It provides a space for relaxation and rejuvenation, allowing you to recharge and approach life's challenges with a greater sense of calmness and clarity.

Embracing mindfulness as a tool for emotional intelligence development can lead to a more fulfilling and balanced life.

Mindfulness as a tool for developing emotional self-awareness and regulation

By incorporating mindfulness practices into your daily routine, you can develop a greater understanding and control of your emotions, allowing you to navigate challenging situations with ease.

For example, imagine you're in a stressful meeting at work and notice yourself becoming overwhelmed. Through mindfulness, you can pause, take a deep breath, and observe your thoughts and emotions without judgment. This allows you to respond calmly and effectively.

Mindfulness serves as a powerful tool for developing emotional self-awareness and regulation. It enables you to become more attuned to your internal states, recognizing the triggers that lead to certain emotions. By cultivating this awareness, you can then regulate your emotions by consciously choosing how to respond rather than react impulsively.

Mindfulness also helps you develop a compassionate and non-judgmental attitude towards yourself and your emotions, fostering self-acceptance and reducing self-criticism. This practice allows you to cultivate a sense of inner calm and resilience, enabling you to navigate the ups and downs of life with greater ease and emotional intelligence.

Combining Emotional Intelligence and Mindfulness Practices

When it comes to combining emotional intelligence and mindfulness practices, there are several key points to consider.

First, integrating mindfulness meditation into emotional intelligence exercises can help individuals develop a greater sense of self-awareness and self-regulation. By incorporating mindfulness techniques, such as focused breathing or body scans, into emotional intelligence activities, you can cultivate a more present and centered state of mind.

Second, using mindfulness to enhance empathy and social skills is another valuable aspect of this combination. Mindfulness encourages individuals to be fully present and attentive in their interactions with others, which can foster deeper connections and understanding. By practicing mindful listening and empathetic response, you can strengthen your ability to relate to and connect with others on a more meaningful level.

Lastly, mindfulness can be a powerful tool for building resilience and managing stress. By incorporating mindfulness practices into your daily routine, such as meditation or mindful movement, you can develop a greater capacity to navigate and cope with challenging emotions and situations. Mindfulness can help you cultivate a sense of calm and equanimity, allowing you to approach stressors with greater clarity and resilience.

Integrating mindfulness meditation into emotional intelligence exercises

Incorporating mindfulness meditation amplifies emotional intelligence exercises, allowing you to cultivate a deeper understanding of your emotions. By integrating mindfulness practices into your emotional intelligence journey, you're able to develop a heightened awareness of your thoughts, feelings, and bodily sensations in the present moment.

This increased self-awareness enables you to recognize and regulate your emotions more effectively, leading to enhanced emotional intelligence. Mindfulness meditation also helps you develop a non-judgmental and compassionate attitude towards yourself and others, fostering empathy and understanding.

Through regular practice, you can learn to observe your emotions without getting caught up in them, allowing you to respond more skillfully in challenging situations. The combination of mindfulness meditation and emotional intelligence exercises creates a powerful synergy, empowering you to navigate and manage your emotions with greater ease and wisdom.

Using mindfulness to enhance empathy and social skills

Now that you've learned how to integrate mindfulness meditation into your emotional intelligence exercises, it's time to take it a step further and explore how mindfulness can enhance your empathy and social skills.

Mindfulness allows you to be fully present and aware of your own emotions, thoughts, and sensations. By cultivating this self-awareness, you become more attuned to the emotions and experiences of others. This heightened sensitivity enables you to empathize with others on a deeper level, understanding their perspectives and connecting with them on a more meaningful level.

Additionally, mindfulness helps you develop better social skills by fostering a non-judgmental attitude and promoting active listening. When you're fully present in the moment and truly listen to others without judgment or distraction, you can engage in more authentic and fulfilling social interactions.

So, by incorporating mindfulness into your daily life, you can strengthen your empathy and social skills, ultimately enhancing your emotional intelligence.

Mindfulness as a tool for building resilience and managing stress

Mindfulness is like a soothing balm for your mind, helping you build resilience and effectively manage stress. By practicing mindfulness, you're able to cultivate a greater awareness of your thoughts, emotions, and physical sensations. This allows you to respond to stressors in a more calm and composed manner.

It provides you with the tools to observe your thoughts without judgment. This, in turn, helps you gain a better understanding of your stress triggers and patterns. Through this understanding, you can develop healthier coping mechanisms and make more conscious choices in how you respond to stress.

Mindfulness also helps you develop a sense of acceptance. This allows you to acknowledge and work through stressful situations rather than becoming overwhelmed by them. By incorporating mindfulness into your daily routine, you can build a strong foundation of resilience and find inner peace amidst life's challenges.

Mindful Living and Emotional Intelligence

When it comes to applying emotional intelligence in your daily life, mindfulness can play a crucial role.

By being present and aware of your emotions, you can make more informed decisions and navigate challenging situations with grace.

Mindful decision-making allows you to consider not only your own emotions, but also the emotions of others, leading to more empathetic and effective outcomes.

Finally, sustaining emotional intelligence through mindfulness practices is essential for long-term growth and well-being.

By regularly practicing mindfulness, you can cultivate self-awareness, manage stress, and maintain healthy relationships.

Applying emotional intelligence in daily life through mindfulness

Start incorporating emotional intelligence into your daily life by practicing mindfulness.

Mindfulness is the practice of being fully present in the moment, paying attention to your thoughts, feelings, and sensations without judgment.

By cultivating mindfulness, you can develop a greater awareness of your emotions and how they impact your daily life.

This awareness allows you to respond to situations with greater clarity and intention, rather than reacting impulsively based on emotional triggers.

As you practice mindfulness, you can begin to observe your emotions without getting caught up in them, which can help you make wiser choices and navigate challenging situations more effectively.

Mindfulness also helps you develop empathy and compassion towards yourself and others, as you learn to understand and accept your own emotions and the emotions of those around you.

By practicing mindfulness regularly, you can strengthen your emotional intelligence and enhance your overall well-being.

Mindful decision-making and emotional intelligence

Now that you've explored the application of emotional intelligence in daily life through mindfulness, it's time to delve into the powerful connection between mindful decision-making and emotional intelligence.

When you approach decision-making with mindfulness, you're not only tapping into your rational thinking but also taking into account your emotions and those of others involved.

By being aware of your emotions and their influence on your decision-making process, you can make choices that align with your values and goals while also considering the impact on yourself and those around you.

Mindful decision-making allows you to navigate through the complexity of emotions, ensuring that your choices are well-informed, compassionate, and in line with your true desires.

It empowers you to make decisions that aren't only logical but also emotionally intelligent, fostering positive outcomes and nurturing healthier relationships.

Sustaining emotional intelligence through mindfulness practices

To truly master the art of sustaining emotional intelligence, you need to embrace mindfulness practices and dive headfirst into the ocean of self-awareness.

By cultivating a mindful approach to your emotions, you can develop a deeper understanding of yourself and those around you.

Mindfulness allows you to observe your thoughts and feelings without judgment, creating a space for self-reflection and growth.

Through practices like meditation and deep breathing, you can anchor yourself in the present moment and become more attuned to your emotions.

This heightened self-awareness enables you to make conscious choices rather than reacting impulsively based on your emotions.

By consistently practicing mindfulness, you can strengthen your emotional intelligence and maintain a healthy balance between your thoughts, feelings, and actions.

So, take a moment to pause, breathe, and connect with yourself. Embrace the power of mindfulness and watch as your emotional intelligence flourishes.

XVI. Emotional Intelligence in the Digital Age

In today's digital age, emotional intelligence plays a crucial role in how we navigate our relationships with technology. It requires a balance between staying connected and mindful of our emotions.

Navigating digital relationships with emotional intelligence helps us establish healthy boundaries and maintain genuine connections, while also promoting self-awareness and empathy.

Similarly, understanding the impact of technology on our overall well-being is essential for maintaining a healthy digital lifestyle. Prioritizing digital wellness through emotional intelligence allows us to manage our screen time, set boundaries, and prioritize our mental and emotional health.

Emotional Intelligence and Technology

In today's digital age, it's crucial to understand the impact of technology on emotional intelligence. With the constant use of screens and devices, challenges arise in developing and maintaining emotional intelligence.

However, amidst these challenges, there are also opportunities for growth and development of emotional intelligence. Technology provides new avenues for self-awareness and empathy.

It's important to find a balance between technology use and emotional well-being. Excessive screen time can hinder social skills and emotional connections.

Understanding the impact of technology on emotional intelligence

Imagine how your emotional intelligence could be affected by the constant presence and reliance on technology in your daily life. The impact of technology on emotional intelligence is a complex and multifaceted issue.

On one hand, technology has provided us with numerous tools and platforms to connect with others, express ourselves, and access information. However, the digital world also poses challenges to our emotional well-being. The constant exposure to social media, for example, can lead to feelings of comparison, inadequacy, and FOMO (fear of missing out).

Additionally, the convenience and efficiency of technology often prioritize productivity over emotional connection, leading to a potential decline in our ability to understand and empathize with others. It is crucial to recognize these potential pitfalls and actively work towards maintaining a healthy balance between technology use and emotional well-being.

By being mindful of our digital habits, setting boundaries, and prioritizing meaningful offline interactions, we can mitigate the negative impact of technology and foster the growth of our emotional intelligence.

Challenges and opportunities for emotional intelligence in the digital age

The digital age presents both obstacles and possibilities for nurturing and enhancing our understanding of others' feelings and fostering meaningful connections.

On one hand, the constant presence of technology in our lives can lead to a sense of disconnection and isolation, as face-to-face interactions are replaced by screens and virtual communication. It can be challenging to accurately interpret emotions through text messages or social media posts, as the nuances of non-verbal cues and tone of voice are lost.

However, the digital age also offers opportunities for emotional intelligence to thrive. Online platforms provide a space for individuals to share their thoughts and feelings openly, creating a sense of community and support. Additionally, advancements in technology, such as virtual reality or artificial intelligence, have the potential to enhance emotional intelligence training and therapy, allowing individuals to practice and develop their empathy skills in a safe and controlled environment.

It is crucial that we navigate the digital landscape with a mindful and compassionate approach, actively seeking out opportunities to connect with others on a deeper emotional level, while also being aware of the limitations and challenges that technology presents.

Balancing technology use with emotional well-being and social skills

In today's digital age, challenges and opportunities arise for emotional intelligence as we navigate the delicate balance between technology use and emotional well-being.

It is essential to recognize the impact of excessive screen time on our mental and social health.

While technology offers convenience and connectivity, it can also lead to feelings of isolation and disconnection from genuine human interactions.

As you strive to maintain emotional well-being and develop strong social skills, it is crucial to strike a balance between the virtual world and the real one.

Allocating time for face-to-face interactions, practicing mindfulness, and setting boundaries with technology can help foster emotional intelligence and strengthen your interpersonal relationships.

Remember, nurturing your emotional well-being is a lifelong journey, and finding harmony between technology and human connection is an integral part of it.

Navigating Digital Relationships with Emotional Intelligence

When it comes to online communication, emotional intelligence plays a crucial role in navigating digital relationships.

Managing emotions in social media interactions is essential for maintaining healthy connections in the digital realm.

Building and maintaining authentic relationships online requires empathy, understanding, and effective communication skills to truly connect with others in a meaningful way.

Emotional intelligence in online communication

Improve your online communication skills by harnessing the power of emotional intelligence, just like a skilled diplomat navigating a delicate negotiation.

In the digital realm, where tone and body language are absent, understanding and managing emotions becomes even more crucial.

By being aware of your own emotions and the emotions of others, you can navigate online conversations with empathy and insight.

Pay attention to the subtle cues and nuances in written messages, such as word choice, punctuation, and even the use of emojis.

Be mindful of how your own words may be interpreted and make an effort to communicate clearly and respectfully.

Practice active listening by truly understanding the perspective of the other person before responding.

By approaching online communication with emotional intelligence, you can build stronger connections, diffuse conflicts, and foster a positive and inclusive online environment.

Managing emotions in social media interactions

Take control of your feelings while engaging in social media interactions by recognizing and managing the subtle cues and nuances in written messages.

Social media platforms have become a breeding ground for miscommunication and misunderstanding, often leading to unnecessary conflicts and hurt feelings.

By honing your emotional intelligence skills, you can navigate these digital spaces with more grace and understanding.

Pay attention to the tone, language, and context of the messages you receive, as they may not always accurately convey the sender's true intentions.

Remember that written words lack the non-verbal cues we rely on in face-to-face interactions, making it easy for emotions to be misinterpreted.

Take a moment to pause before responding, allowing yourself time to process your emotions and respond in a thoughtful manner.

Practice empathy and consider the perspective of the other person before jumping to conclusions.

By managing your emotions and responding with empathy, you can foster healthier and more meaningful social media interactions.

Building and maintaining authentic relationships in the digital realm

Now that you've learned how to manage your emotions in social media interactions, it's time to focus on building and maintaining authentic relationships in the digital realm.

In a world where online connections have become the norm, it's crucial to approach these relationships with intention and authenticity. The key lies in being genuine and transparent, allowing others to see the real you behind the screen.

By engaging in meaningful conversations, actively listening, and showing empathy, you can forge deeper connections that go beyond superficial interactions. Remember, the digital realm can sometimes feel disconnected and impersonal, but by bringing your authentic self to the table, you have the power to create and nurture relationships that are both meaningful and fulfilling.

Emotional Intelligence and Digital Wellness

When it comes to setting boundaries and managing digital distractions with emotional intelligence, you'll find that it's all about finding the right balance.

By being aware of your emotional needs and using your emotional intelligence, you can navigate the digital world in a way that supports your overall well-being.

Additionally, technology mindfulness can be a powerful tool for enhancing emotional well-being. By practicing mindfulness while using technology, you can cultivate a greater sense of presence and awareness, allowing you to better manage your emotions and maintain a healthy relationship with digital devices.

Lastly, technology can also be used as a tool for developing emotional intelligence. From online resources to apps and programs specifically designed for emotional well-being, technology can provide valuable tools and resources to help you develop and strengthen your emotional intelligence skills.

Setting boundaries and managing digital distractions with emotional intelligence

Establishing healthy boundaries and effectively managing digital distractions is crucial for enhancing your emotional intelligence and maintaining a balanced lifestyle. In today's fast-paced, technology-driven world, it's easy to get caught up in the constant stream of notifications, emails, and social media updates.

However, constantly being plugged in can lead to feelings of overwhelm, stress, and a lack of focus. By setting boundaries and being mindful of your digital usage, you can create space for deeper self-reflection, improved relationships, and increased productivity.

It's important to recognize when you need to step away from your devices and engage in activities that promote relaxation and connection, such as spending time in nature, practicing mindfulness, or engaging in face-to-face conversations.

Additionally, practicing emotional intelligence can help you better understand and manage your emotions in relation to your digital distractions. By being aware of how your digital habits affect your emotional well-being, you can make conscious choices that align with your values and priorities.

Remember, it's okay to take breaks, set limits, and prioritize your mental and emotional health. By doing so, you can cultivate a healthier relationship with technology and enhance your overall emotional intelligence.

Enhancing emotional well-being through technology mindfulness

To enhance your emotional well-being, it's essential to cultivate mindfulness in your use of technology.

In today's fast-paced world, it's easy to get caught up in the constant stream of information and notifications that technology provides. However, constantly being connected can take a toll on your emotional state.

By practicing technology mindfulness, you can create a healthier relationship with your devices and improve your overall well-being.

Start by setting boundaries and creating designated times for technology use, allowing yourself to disconnect and focus on other aspects of your life.

Additionally, be aware of how certain apps or social media platforms make you feel and consider limiting your exposure to those that bring about negative emotions.

Take breaks from screens throughout the day, engaging in activities that promote relaxation and connection with the present moment.

By being mindful of your technology use, you can foster a sense of balance and emotional well-being in your life.

Using technology as a tool for emotional intelligence development

Now that you've learned about enhancing emotional well-being through technology mindfulness, it's time to explore how technology can be used as a tool for developing emotional intelligence.

In today's digital age, we're constantly surrounded by various technological devices and applications that can help us better understand and manage our emotions. From mood tracking apps to virtual reality simulations, technology offers a multitude of resources that can support our emotional growth and self-awareness.

By utilizing these tools, you can gain insights into your emotional patterns, learn effective strategies for emotional regulation, and even practice empathy and compassion in virtual scenarios. Technology has the potential to provide us with a safe and accessible environment for honing our emotional intelligence skills, ultimately leading to a more fulfilling and harmonious life.

XVII. Emotional Intelligence and Success

Emotional intelligence plays a crucial role in achieving professional success. By understanding and managing your own emotions, as well as accurately perceiving and relating to the emotions of others, you can navigate workplace dynamics with greater ease and effectiveness.

Additionally, emotional intelligence is key to achieving personal success as it helps you build strong relationships, communicate effectively, and make sound decisions, all of which are essential in reaching your goals.

Emotional Intelligence and Professional Success

If you want to succeed in your career, it's essential to understand the impact of emotional intelligence.

Emotional intelligence plays a crucial role in career progression by helping individuals navigate challenging situations, communicate effectively, and build strong relationships with colleagues.

Additionally, emotional intelligence is particularly important in leadership and management roles, as it enables leaders to inspire and motivate their teams, make sound decisions, and handle conflicts with empathy and understanding.

Lastly, emotional intelligence also plays a significant role in entrepreneurial success, as it helps entrepreneurs navigate uncertainty, build strong networks, and understand and meet the needs of their customers.

The impact of emotional intelligence on career progression

With a high level of emotional intelligence, you can navigate your career path like a skilled pilot guiding a plane through turbulence.

Emotional intelligence plays a crucial role in the progression of your career.

It allows you to understand and manage your own emotions effectively, which in turn helps you navigate challenging situations and relationships at work. By being aware of your emotions and how they impact your behavior, you can make better decisions, communicate more effectively, and build strong professional relationships.

Additionally, emotional intelligence enables you to empathize with your colleagues and understand their perspectives, fostering a positive work environment and collaborative culture. As you progress in your career, your ability to handle stress, adapt to changes, and effectively manage conflicts becomes increasingly important.

By developing and honing your emotional intelligence skills, you can position yourself for success and unlock your full potential in the professional world.

Emotional intelligence in leadership and management roles

Step into a leadership role and watch as your ability to understand and connect with others on a deeper level propels your team to new heights.

As a leader, your emotional intelligence plays a crucial role in effectively managing and inspiring your team. By being aware of your own emotions and those of others, you can create a positive and supportive work environment that fosters collaboration and productivity.

Your ability to empathize with your team members allows you to address their needs and concerns, leading to increased trust and loyalty. Additionally, your emotional intelligence enables you to navigate conflicts and difficult situations with grace and understanding, finding solutions that benefit everyone involved.

By harnessing the power of emotional intelligence in your leadership and management roles, you can create a harmonious and successful work environment that brings out the best in your team.

Emotional intelligence and entrepreneurial success

Improve your chances of entrepreneurial success by honing your ability to understand and connect with others on a deeper level.

Emotional intelligence plays a crucial role in the world of entrepreneurship, as it allows you to build strong relationships, motivate your team, and navigate through various challenges.

By being emotionally intelligent, you can effectively communicate with your employees, clients, and investors, understanding their needs and concerns. This insight enables you to make informed decisions and adapt your business strategies accordingly.

Additionally, emotional intelligence allows you to empathize with others, creating a positive work environment and fostering collaboration. It also helps you manage stress and handle setbacks, allowing you to bounce back from failures and maintain resilience.

Overall, developing emotional intelligence is essential for entrepreneurial success, as it empowers you to forge meaningful connections, inspire others, and navigate the ever-changing landscape of business with confidence.

Achieving Personal Success through Emotional Intelligence

If you want to achieve personal success, you need to utilize emotional intelligence in setting and achieving your goals.

By understanding and managing your emotions, you can develop effective strategies that align with your values and aspirations.

Additionally, emotional intelligence helps you overcome setbacks and obstacles by allowing you to adapt and bounce back from challenges with resilience and determination.

Lastly, by leveraging emotional intelligence, you can foster personal and professional growth as you build strong relationships, make better decisions, and lead with empathy and authenticity.

Strategies for setting and achieving goals with emotional intelligence

Ironically, when you don't set goals and ignore emotional intelligence, you're practically begging for failure. Setting and achieving goals requires not only a clear vision but also the ability to understand and manage your emotions along the way.

Emotional intelligence plays a crucial role in helping you stay focused, motivated, and resilient in the face of challenges. By harnessing your emotional intelligence, you can develop effective strategies for goal setting and achievement.

Start by identifying your values and passions, as they'll provide the foundation for your goals. Then, break your goals down into achievable steps and create a timeline to keep yourself on track. It's important to be flexible and open to adjusting your goals as circumstances change.

Additionally, practice self-awareness by recognizing and managing any negative emotions that may hinder your progress. Use positive affirmations, visualization techniques, and self-reflection to stay motivated and overcome obstacles.

Remember, emotional intelligence isn't just about understanding and managing your own emotions; it also involves empathy and understanding others' emotions. By incorporating empathy into your goal-setting process, you can build strong relationships and collaborate effectively with others.

So, set your goals with emotional intelligence in mind, and watch as you achieve personal success and fulfillment.

Overcoming setbacks and obstacles through emotional intelligence

By harnessing your ability to understand and manage your emotions, you can navigate through setbacks and obstacles with resilience and determination, ultimately achieving personal growth and triumph.

Life is full of unexpected challenges that can throw us off course and make us question our abilities. However, by cultivating emotional intelligence, you can develop the necessary tools to overcome these hurdles.

When faced with a setback, take a moment to acknowledge the emotions that arise and allow yourself to process them. By doing so, you can gain a clearer perspective and make more rational decisions.

Additionally, it's important to practice self-compassion during these difficult times. Remind yourself that setbacks are a natural part of the journey towards success and that everyone experiences them at some point.

Use setbacks as an opportunity to learn and grow, rather than allowing them to define your worth or capabilities.

Finally, surround yourself with a support system of friends, family, or mentors who can provide guidance and encouragement. Their perspective and advice can offer valuable insights and help you navigate through obstacles.

Remember that setbacks are not permanent, and with emotional intelligence, you have the power to overcome them and continue on your path towards personal growth and triumph.

Leveraging emotional intelligence for personal and professional growth

So, you've managed to overcome setbacks and obstacles through emotional intelligence, and now it's time to take it a step further. By leveraging your emotional intelligence, you've got the power to fuel your personal and professional growth.

In today's fast-paced world, it's not just about IQ or technical skills anymore; emotional intelligence plays a crucial role in determining success. It allows you to understand and manage your emotions effectively, communicate with others empathetically, and navigate through challenging situations with grace.

By honing your emotional intelligence, you can build stronger relationships, inspire others, and make better decisions. It's a skill that can truly transform your life, both personally and professionally.

So, embrace the power of emotional intelligence and watch yourself grow in ways you never thought possible.

XVIII. Emotional Intelligence and Mental Health

When it comes to mental health, emotional intelligence plays a crucial role in understanding and managing our emotions effectively.

By developing emotional intelligence, you can gain insights into your own mental well-being and take proactive steps to maintain it.

Additionally, emotional intelligence can help you recognize when you need support and seek it from others, fostering a healthier mindset and overall mental health.

The Connection between Emotional Intelligence and Mental Health

Emotional intelligence plays a crucial role as a protective factor for your mental health. By developing emotional intelligence skills, you can effectively manage and navigate through various mental health challenges. These skills enable you to recognize and understand your own emotions, as well as empathize with others, ultimately fostering resilience in the face of mental health difficulties.

Emotional intelligence as a protective factor for mental health

By tapping into your emotional intelligence, you can unlock the key to safeguarding your mental well-being like a shield against the storms of life.

Emotional intelligence acts as a protective factor for your mental health, allowing you to navigate and manage the challenges and difficulties that come your way.

When you're emotionally intelligent, you have a greater understanding of your own emotions and can regulate them effectively. This self-awareness and self-management enable you to respond to stressful situations in a healthier and more adaptive manner, reducing the negative impact on your mental health.

Additionally, emotional intelligence allows you to empathize with others, fostering positive relationships and social support networks that contribute to your overall well-being.

By developing your emotional intelligence, you can strengthen your resilience, enhance your coping mechanisms, and create a solid foundation for your mental health.

So, embrace your emotional intelligence and harness its power to protect and nurture your mental well-being.

Emotional intelligence skills for managing mental health challenges

Now that you understand the importance of emotional intelligence as a protective factor for mental health, it's time to delve into the specific skills that can help you manage any challenges you may be facing.

Developing emotional intelligence skills can provide you with valuable tools to navigate the ups and downs of your mental health journey. By honing your ability to identify and understand your own emotions, you can gain insight into what triggers certain mental health challenges and develop strategies to cope with them effectively.

Additionally, being able to empathize and connect with others on an emotional level can create a support system that is essential for your well-being. These skills allow you to communicate your needs and seek the help and understanding you deserve.

By actively engaging in the development of emotional intelligence, you're taking an important step towards managing your mental health challenges and building a more resilient and fulfilling life.

Emotional intelligence and resilience in the face of mental health difficulties

Developing strong emotional intelligence skills can help you build resilience and navigate the challenges of mental health with greater ease. When faced with mental health difficulties, having a high level of emotional intelligence allows you to understand and manage your emotions effectively. It enables you to recognize and address negative thought patterns, regulate your emotions, and cope with stress in a healthy way.

By developing emotional intelligence, you can cultivate a greater sense of self-awareness, which is crucial in identifying and addressing the underlying causes of your mental health challenges. Additionally, emotional intelligence helps you build strong relationships and support networks, providing you with the necessary emotional support during difficult times.

By developing these skills, you can better cope with the ups and downs of mental health, bounce back from setbacks, and maintain a positive outlook on life.

Emotional Intelligence Strategies for Mental Well-Being

In this discussion, we'll explore some key points on how emotional intelligence can be used as a tool for stress management.

By developing your emotional intelligence, you can learn effective coping mechanisms for dealing with anxiety and depression. This will allow you to navigate these challenges more effectively.

Furthermore, emotional intelligence can help enhance your self-care and self-compassion. This enables you to prioritize your mental well-being and nurture a healthier relationship with yourself.

Emotional intelligence tools for stress management

One effective tool for stress management is using emotional intelligence. When faced with stress, it's important to recognize and understand your emotions in order to effectively manage them.

Emotional intelligence allows you to identify and regulate your emotions, which can help you navigate through challenging situations with clarity and composure. By being aware of your emotional state, you can develop strategies to cope with stress, such as practicing mindfulness, engaging in self-care activities, and seeking support from others.

Additionally, emotional intelligence enables you to empathize with others who may also be experiencing stress, fostering connection and understanding. By using emotional intelligence as a tool for stress management, you can not only reduce your own stress levels but also cultivate healthy relationships and promote overall mental well-being.

Coping with anxiety and depression through emotional intelligence

Take control of your anxiety and depression by tapping into your inner strength and understanding your own emotions. It's essential to recognize that anxiety and depression are complex and multifaceted, but with emotional intelligence, you can develop effective coping strategies.

Start by acknowledging and accepting your emotions without judgment or self-criticism. Allow yourself to feel, explore, and express these emotions in a healthy and constructive way. Embrace self-awareness by understanding the triggers and patterns that contribute to your anxiety and depression. By identifying the root causes, you can work towards resolving them and preventing future episodes.

Additionally, practice self-compassion and self-care to nurture your emotional well-being. Engage in activities that bring you joy, relaxation, and fulfillment. Surround yourself with a supportive network of friends, family, or professionals who can offer guidance and understanding.

Remember, you have the power to transform your emotional landscape and find inner peace.

Enhancing self-care and self-compassion with emotional intelligence

Now that you've learned how emotional intelligence can help you cope with anxiety and depression, let's explore how it can enhance your self-care and self-compassion.

Taking care of yourself is essential for your overall well-being, and emotional intelligence can be a powerful tool in this process. By developing emotional intelligence, you'll become more attuned to your own needs and emotions. This will allow you to identify when you need to take a break, practice self-care, or seek support.

Moreover, emotional intelligence helps you cultivate self-compassion, which is crucial for treating yourself with kindness and understanding, especially during challenging times. By harnessing the power of emotional intelligence, you can create a nurturing and compassionate relationship with yourself. This will lead to increased self-care and overall well-being.

Remember, your emotional well-being matters, and emotional intelligence can be a valuable ally in your journey towards self-care and self-compassion.

Emotional Intelligence and Seeking Support

When it comes to seeking support for your mental health, recognizing when to seek professional help is crucial.

Emotional intelligence plays a significant role in navigating therapy and counseling effectively.

With emotional intelligence, you can build a support network that understands and supports your emotional needs, providing a safe and empathetic environment for your mental well-being.

Recognizing when to seek professional help with mental health

Sometimes it's essential to reach out to a professional when our mental wellbeing could use some expert guidance.

Recognizing when to seek professional help with mental health is a crucial step in taking care of ourselves.

It's important to understand that seeking professional help doesn't mean you're weak or incapable of handling your emotions. In fact, it shows strength and self-awareness to recognize when you need additional support.

Professional therapists and counselors are trained to provide the necessary tools and techniques to help individuals navigate through their mental health challenges. They can offer a safe and non-judgmental space for you to express your thoughts and feelings, and provide guidance in developing coping strategies and improving emotional intelligence.

Remember, seeking professional help is a sign of self-care and should be seen as an investment in your overall wellbeing.

Emotional intelligence in navigating therapy and counseling

Developing a strong sense of self-awareness and an understanding of your own emotional needs can greatly enhance your experience in therapy and counseling. When you have a clear understanding of your emotions and how they impact your thoughts and behaviors, you can more effectively communicate with your therapist or counselor about what you need from them.

This self-awareness allows you to articulate your goals, preferences, and boundaries, ensuring that the therapeutic relationship is tailored to your specific needs. Additionally, being in tune with your emotions can help you navigate the ups and downs of the therapeutic process. You can identify when certain topics or approaches resonate with you, and when something doesn't feel quite right.

This insight enables you to actively participate in your own healing journey, making therapy and counseling more collaborative and empowering. Ultimately, emotional intelligence empowers you to take ownership of your mental health and get the most out of your therapeutic experience.

Building a support network with emotional intelligence

Building a strong support network with emotional awareness can greatly enhance your overall well-being and provide you with a valuable source of comfort and understanding.

When you cultivate relationships with people who possess emotional intelligence, you create a safe space where you can freely express your thoughts and feelings without fear of judgment. These individuals have the ability to empathize with your experiences and offer insights that can help you navigate through challenging situations.

By surrounding yourself with emotionally intelligent people, you gain access to different perspectives and coping strategies, allowing you to develop a deeper understanding of yourself and others. Moreover, a support network built on emotional intelligence can provide validation and reassurance, reminding you that you're not alone in your struggles.

The empathetic and insightful guidance from these individuals can empower you to make positive changes in your life and foster personal growth.

XIX. Emotional Intelligence in Education

In the educational setting, emotional intelligence plays a crucial role in shaping the overall well-being and success of students. Educators can help students develop self-awareness, empathy, and effective communication skills by nurturing emotional intelligence.

In the digital learning environment, it becomes even more important to prioritize emotional intelligence as students navigate virtual interactions and face unique challenges.

Emotional Intelligence in Educational Settings

In educational settings, emotional intelligence plays a crucial role in shaping students' experiences and overall success.

Understanding and managing one's emotions can greatly impact academic performance, as it enables students to regulate stress, build resilience, and enhance problem-solving skills.

Furthermore, emotional intelligence also influences classroom dynamics by fostering empathy, effective communication, and positive relationships between teachers and students.

The importance of emotional intelligence in education

Emotional intelligence plays a crucial role in education, as it helps students develop self-awareness and empathy, leading to better communication and problem-solving skills.

For example, imagine a scenario where a student utilizes their emotional intelligence to understand their classmate's feelings of frustration and offers support. By recognizing and empathizing with their peer's emotions, this student creates a safe and supportive learning environment, where everyone feels understood and valued.

Moreover, emotional intelligence enables students to effectively communicate their own needs and concerns, facilitating constructive dialogue and collaboration with their teachers and peers. This heightened level of self-awareness and empathy not only enhances the overall learning experience but also equips students with essential life skills that extend beyond the classroom.

In essence, emotional intelligence is not just a soft skill, but a vital component of education that fosters emotional well-being, resilience, and success in all aspects of life.

Emotional intelligence and academic success

Boost your academic success by developing your ability to understand and manage your emotions effectively. Emotional intelligence plays a crucial role in your academic journey, as it allows you to navigate challenges, build resilience, and maintain a positive mindset.

By being aware of your emotions, you can identify any barriers that may be hindering your learning process and find effective strategies to overcome them. Moreover, managing your emotions enables you to handle stress, anxiety, and pressure more effectively, allowing you to stay focused and perform at your best.

Developing emotional intelligence also enhances your interpersonal skills, enabling you to build stronger relationships with your peers and teachers. This leads to a more supportive and collaborative learning environment, where you can thrive academically.

So, take the time to develop your emotional intelligence and watch as it positively impacts your academic success.

The role of emotional intelligence in classroom dynamics

Improve your academic journey by honing your ability to understand and manage the emotional climate in your classroom, fostering a positive and collaborative learning environment.

Classroom dynamics play a crucial role in shaping the overall educational experience. When students feel safe, supported, and valued, they're more likely to engage actively in the learning process and perform better academically.

Emotional intelligence, which involves recognizing and regulating emotions in oneself and others, is a key factor in creating a positive classroom atmosphere. By developing your emotional intelligence, you can effectively navigate conflicts, promote empathy, and encourage open communication among your peers.

Understanding and addressing the emotional needs of your classmates can also enhance collaboration, teamwork, and mutual respect. By fostering a positive emotional climate in your classroom, you contribute to a conducive learning environment that boosts academic success and personal growth.

Nurturing Emotional Intelligence in Students

In order to promote emotional intelligence in the classroom, it's important to implement strategies that encourage students to recognize and regulate their emotions.

By creating a safe and supportive environment, students can develop their emotional awareness and learn how to effectively manage their behavior.

Additionally, adopting an emotional intelligence-based approach to discipline and behavior management can help students understand the consequences of their actions and develop empathy for others.

Finally, fostering emotional intelligence in academic and career decision-making can empower students to make informed choices based on their emotions and values, leading to greater personal and professional fulfillment.

Strategies for promoting emotional intelligence in the classroom

Enhance your classroom environment by implementing strategies that foster emotional intelligence. By creating a safe and inclusive space where students feel valued and understood, you can help them develop their emotional intelligence.

Encourage open communication and active listening, allowing students to express their thoughts and feelings without fear of judgment. Incorporate activities that promote self-awareness and empathy, such as journaling or group discussions about emotions and perspectives.

Teach conflict resolution and problem-solving skills to empower students to handle conflicts in a healthy and constructive manner. Model and reinforce positive behaviors, like empathy and kindness, and provide opportunities for students to practice these skills through collaborative projects and community service.

Remember, emotional intelligence is just as crucial as academic knowledge, and by prioritizing it in your classroom, you can help students thrive both academically and emotionally.

Emotional intelligence-based approaches to discipline and behavior management

By embracing approaches that prioritize understanding and empathy, you can create a transformative classroom environment where discipline becomes an opportunity for growth and connection.

Instead of resorting to punitive measures, emotional intelligence-based approaches to discipline and behavior management focus on addressing the underlying emotions and needs of students.

This approach recognizes that misbehavior is often a result of unmet emotional needs, and seeks to address those needs rather than simply punishing the behavior.

By taking the time to understand the emotions and triggers behind a student's behavior, you can guide them towards healthier ways of expressing themselves and managing their emotions.

This not only helps to improve their behavior in the long run, but also fosters a sense of trust and connection between you and your students.

Building emotional intelligence in the classroom not only benefits individual students, but also creates a positive and supportive learning environment for all.

Fostering emotional intelligence in academic and career decision-making

When you navigate the path of academic and career decision-making, you become the composer orchestrating the symphony of your future, weaving together the harmonies of your passions, strengths, and aspirations.

It is a journey that requires emotional intelligence, the ability to recognize and understand your own emotions, as well as the emotions of others. By fostering emotional intelligence in this process, you can make decisions that align with your authentic self and bring fulfillment and success.

Emotional intelligence allows you to tap into your intuition, to listen to the whispers of your heart and the guidance of your emotions. It empowers you to make choices that are not solely driven by external expectations or societal pressures, but rather by a deep understanding of what truly matters to you.

When you cultivate emotional intelligence, you develop the capacity to evaluate your options with clarity and discernment. You become attuned to the subtle signals that indicate whether a particular academic or career path will bring you joy, fulfillment, and a sense of purpose.

Moreover, emotional intelligence enables you to navigate the inevitable challenges and setbacks that may arise along the way. It equips you with the resilience and adaptability needed to bounce back from failures, learn from them, and continue moving forward.

By fostering emotional intelligence in academic and career decision-making, you not only enhance your own well-being and success but also contribute to a more harmonious and empathetic society.

Emotional Intelligence in the Digital Learning Environment

In the digital learning environment, it's crucial to adapt emotional intelligence strategies to ensure students' well-being and success.

As an educator, you play a vital role in managing emotions and building resilience in virtual classrooms.

By creating a supportive and empathetic online space, you can empower students to develop their emotional intelligence, helping them navigate the challenges and demands of a digital world.

Adapting emotional intelligence strategies for online learning

Adapting emotional intelligence strategies for online learning is crucial for creating an engaging and effective virtual education experience.

As an online learner, you may face unique challenges such as isolation, lack of face-to-face interaction, and increased screen time.

However, by incorporating emotional intelligence into your online learning journey, you can navigate these challenges more effectively.

By being aware of your emotions and the emotions of others, you can build strong virtual connections, foster a sense of belonging, and promote collaboration.

Additionally, practicing self-regulation can help you manage distractions, maintain focus, and stay motivated in your online learning environment.

Developing empathy and understanding towards your peers can also enhance your ability to communicate effectively and resolve conflicts virtually.

Ultimately, by embracing emotional intelligence strategies in your online learning experience, you can create a supportive and inclusive virtual classroom that promotes growth, engagement, and success.

Managing emotions and building resilience in virtual classrooms

Managing emotions and building resilience in virtual classrooms is essential for creating a supportive and inclusive online learning environment.

In the virtual world, students may face various challenges that can affect their emotions and overall well-being. It's crucial to acknowledge and address these emotions to ensure that students feel supported and understood.

Building resilience is also vital as it equips students with the ability to bounce back from setbacks and adapt to new situations.

By providing tools and strategies to manage emotions and build resilience, educators can create a space where students feel empowered to navigate the virtual classroom with confidence and success.

Empowering students to develop their emotional intelligence in a digital world

Developing emotional intelligence in the digital world is crucial for students' success. Studies show that individuals with higher emotional intelligence are 58% more likely to succeed in their careers. In today's technologically-driven society, students are constantly exposed to digital platforms and virtual classrooms. This makes it essential for them to navigate and understand their emotions in this digital landscape.

Empowering students to develop their emotional intelligence in this digital world is not only about teaching them how to use technology effectively. It is also about helping them understand and manage their emotions in this new context. It's important to provide students with the tools and resources to recognize and express their emotions in a healthy way. Additionally, building resilience in the face of challenges that may arise in the digital realm is crucial.

By fostering emotional intelligence in the digital world, we can equip students with the skills they need to succeed academically, socially, and professionally. It also helps them navigate the complexities of the digital age with confidence and empathy.

XX. Emotional Intelligence in Healthcare

In the healthcare setting, emotional intelligence plays a crucial role in providing effective care and building positive relationships with patients. By enhancing emotional intelligence in healthcare practice, healthcare professionals can better understand and connect with their patients on an emotional level, leading to improved patient outcomes and satisfaction.

Additionally, emotional intelligence is essential in multidisciplinary healthcare teams, as it facilitates effective communication, collaboration, and empathy among team members, ultimately enhancing the quality of care provided to patients.

Emotional Intelligence in Healthcare Settings

In healthcare settings, emotional intelligence plays a significant role in the effectiveness of healthcare professionals. Your ability to understand and manage your own emotions, as well as empathize with patients, can greatly impact the level of patient satisfaction.

Additionally, studies have shown that emotional intelligence can also have a direct impact on healthcare outcomes. Healthcare professionals who possess high emotional intelligence are better equipped to handle stressful situations and communicate effectively with patients, leading to improved overall outcomes.

The significance of emotional intelligence in healthcare professionals

Emotional intelligence plays a crucial role in the effectiveness and compassion of healthcare professionals. As a healthcare professional, your ability to understand and manage your own emotions, as well as empathize with the emotions of others, is essential in providing quality care to patients.

When you're able to recognize and regulate your own emotions, it allows you to remain calm and composed in stressful situations, which can be incredibly beneficial in a fast-paced and high-pressure healthcare environment.

Additionally, having a high level of emotional intelligence enables you to connect with patients on a deeper level, understanding their fears, concerns, and needs, and providing them with the support and comfort they require.

By being attuned to the emotions of both yourself and your patients, you are better equipped to provide compassionate care that addresses not only their physical ailments but also their emotional well-being.

Emotional intelligence and patient satisfaction

Patient satisfaction is directly influenced by your ability as a healthcare professional to understand and address the emotional needs of your patients, leading to improved overall experiences and outcomes.

For example, a study conducted at a hospital found that patients who felt you genuinely cared about their emotional well-being reported higher levels of satisfaction and were more likely to follow their prescribed treatment plans.

This highlights the importance of emotional intelligence in healthcare, as it allows you to connect with your patients on a deeper level, providing them with the support and empathy they need during their healthcare journey.

By recognizing and addressing their emotional needs, you can create a more positive and personalized experience, ultimately leading to better patient outcomes and satisfaction.

The impact of emotional intelligence on healthcare outcomes

By understanding and addressing the emotional needs of those in your care, you can greatly impact the overall outcome of their healthcare journey. Emotional intelligence plays a crucial role in healthcare outcomes as it allows healthcare providers to connect with patients on a deeper level, fostering trust and rapport.

When patients feel understood and supported emotionally, they're more likely to actively participate in their treatment plans, adhere to medication regimens, and engage in healthy behaviors. Additionally, emotional intelligence enables healthcare providers to effectively communicate and empathize with patients, which can lead to better patient satisfaction and improved patient-provider relationships.

Furthermore, research has shown that healthcare providers with higher levels of emotional intelligence are better equipped to manage stress, handle difficult situations, and prevent burnout.

In conclusion, by incorporating emotional intelligence into healthcare practice, professionals can positively influence the overall well-being and outcomes of their patients.

Enhancing Emotional Intelligence in Healthcare Practice

When it comes to enhancing emotional intelligence in healthcare practice, it's crucial to focus on developing skills for effective communication with patients.

Being able to understand and regulate your own emotions, as well as empathize with the emotions of others, can greatly improve the patient-provider relationship.

Additionally, empathy and compassion play a vital role in healthcare, and cultivating these qualities through emotional intelligence can lead to better patient outcomes and satisfaction.

Lastly, it's important for healthcare professionals to practice emotional self-care, as the demands of the job can be emotionally draining.

Taking the time to prioritize self-care and manage stress can ultimately contribute to better patient care and overall job satisfaction.

Emotional intelligence skills for effective communication with patients

Developing strong emotional intelligence skills is essential for healthcare professionals to effectively communicate with and understand their patients. By honing these skills, you can create a safe and supportive environment where patients feel heard, valued, and understood.

Active listening plays a crucial role in effective communication, as it allows you to fully engage with patients, comprehend their concerns, and respond empathetically. Additionally, being able to recognize and manage your own emotions can help you navigate challenging situations and maintain professionalism.

Understanding nonverbal cues, such as body language and facial expressions, can also provide valuable insights into a patient's emotional state.

By actively working on enhancing your emotional intelligence skills, you can build strong connections with your patients, improve patient satisfaction, and ultimately provide better healthcare outcomes.

Empathy and compassion in healthcare through emotional intelligence

Healthcare professionals who possess strong emotional intelligence skills are able to deeply connect with their patients, fostering empathy and compassion that can make a world of difference in patient care.

By understanding and empathizing with the emotions and experiences of their patients, healthcare professionals can create a safe and supportive environment where patients feel understood and cared for. This can lead to better communication, increased patient satisfaction, and improved healthcare outcomes.

When healthcare professionals demonstrate compassion, patients feel validated and reassured, which can alleviate anxiety and improve overall well-being.

Emotional intelligence also allows healthcare professionals to recognize and respond to the emotional needs of their patients, providing comfort and support during difficult times.

By incorporating emotional intelligence into their practice, healthcare professionals can truly make a positive impact on the lives of their patients.

Emotional self-care for healthcare professionals

Now that we've explored the importance of empathy and compassion in healthcare through emotional intelligence, let's shift our focus to the concept of emotional self-care for healthcare professionals.

As a healthcare professional, taking care of yourself emotionally is crucial in order to provide the best care for your patients. It's easy to get caught up in the demands of your work, constantly putting others' needs before your own. However, neglecting your own emotional well-being can lead to burnout and hinder your ability to effectively connect with and support your patients.

By prioritizing emotional self-care, you can recharge and replenish your own emotional reserves, allowing you to approach your work with renewed energy and compassion. This can be achieved through activities such as self-reflection, seeking support from colleagues or therapists, engaging in hobbies or activities that bring you joy, and setting boundaries to protect your own emotional space.

Remember, taking care of yourself isn't selfish, but rather a necessary step towards providing the best care possible for others.

Emotional Intelligence in Multidisciplinary Healthcare Teams

In collaborative healthcare settings, emotional intelligence plays a crucial role in fostering effective teamwork and communication among multidisciplinary teams.

By understanding and managing their own emotions and those of their team members, healthcare professionals can navigate conflicts and challenges more effectively, leading to improved patient outcomes.

Additionally, emotional intelligence enables healthcare teams to provide patient-centered care by empathizing with patients' emotions, needs, and preferences, ultimately enhancing the overall quality of care.

Emotional intelligence in collaborative healthcare settings

Collaborative healthcare settings thrive when team members possess high emotional intelligence. In these settings, it's crucial for healthcare professionals to be able to effectively communicate, collaborate, and empathize with one another.

Emotional intelligence allows individuals to understand and manage their own emotions, as well as recognize and respond to the emotions of others. This level of awareness and empathy fosters a supportive and cohesive team environment, where trust and open communication can flourish.

When team members are able to regulate their emotions and effectively navigate conflicts, they can work together more efficiently and provide better patient care. Additionally, emotional intelligence enables healthcare professionals to connect with patients on a deeper level, enhancing the therapeutic relationship and ultimately improving patient outcomes.

By prioritizing emotional intelligence in collaborative healthcare settings, teams can create a positive and harmonious work environment that benefits both the professionals and the patients they serve.

Emotional intelligence and conflict resolution in healthcare teams

To effectively resolve conflicts in healthcare teams, you must understand that 'where there's smoke, there's fire.' Conflict is often an indication of underlying issues or unmet needs within the team.

It is crucial to approach conflict resolution with emotional intelligence, which involves recognizing and understanding emotions, both your own and those of others. By acknowledging and validating emotions, you create a safe space for open communication and collaboration.

Active listening is essential in conflict resolution, as it allows you to fully grasp the concerns and perspectives of all team members involved.

Empathy plays a significant role in conflict resolution, as it enables you to put yourself in others' shoes and understand their experiences and emotions.

By practicing emotional intelligence, you can foster effective conflict resolution in healthcare teams, leading to improved teamwork, communication, and ultimately, better patient care.

Promoting patient-centered care through emotional intelligence

Developing your ability to understand and connect with patients on an emotional level can greatly enhance the quality of care you provide. Patient-centered care is not just about treating the physical symptoms, but also addressing the emotional needs of patients. By utilizing emotional intelligence, healthcare professionals can create a safe and supportive environment where patients feel heard, understood, and valued.

This can lead to improved patient satisfaction, increased adherence to treatment plans, and better health outcomes. When you're able to empathize with your patients, you can better understand their fears, anxieties, and concerns, allowing you to tailor your approach to meet their individual needs. This can result in a more personalized and effective care plan, fostering a sense of trust and collaboration between you and your patients.

Additionally, emotional intelligence can also help you navigate difficult conversations and resolve conflicts in a respectful and compassionate manner. By recognizing and managing your own emotions, as well as understanding and responding to the emotions of others, you can promote open communication and build stronger relationships with your patients.

Ultimately, by incorporating emotional intelligence into your practice, you can truly make a difference in the lives of your patients and provide them with the highest level of patient-centered care.

XXI. The Role of Emotional Intelligence in Conflict Transformation

In this subtopic, you'll explore the role of emotional intelligence in conflict transformation. You'll learn about how emotional intelligence can be a powerful tool in resolving conflicts by understanding and managing emotions effectively.

Additionally, you'll discover various strategies that utilize emotional intelligence to transform conflicts into opportunities for growth and understanding.

Conflict Transformation and Emotional Intelligence

In this discussion, you'll explore the connection between conflict transformation and emotional intelligence. You'll delve into the definition of conflict transformation and its relationship with emotional intelligence. You'll also examine the principles that guide emotionally intelligent conflict transformation.

Furthermore, you'll examine the potential of emotional intelligence in facilitating sustainable resolutions to conflicts. By delving into these key points, you'll gain insight into how emotional intelligence plays a vital role in navigating and resolving conflicts effectively.

Defining conflict transformation and its relationship with emotional intelligence

To truly understand conflict transformation and its connection to emotional intelligence, you need to recognize that 85% of workplace conflicts are rooted in unresolved emotional issues. It's not just about the surface-level disagreements or differences in opinion; there are often deep-seated emotions that fuel these conflicts.

Emotional intelligence plays a crucial role in conflict transformation because it allows individuals to understand and manage their own emotions, as well as empathize with the emotions of others. By developing emotional intelligence, you can become more self-aware and better equipped to navigate conflicts in a constructive manner. This involves recognizing your own triggers, being able to regulate your emotions, and effectively communicating your needs and concerns.

Additionally, emotional intelligence enables you to empathize with others, understand their perspectives, and find common ground. By addressing the emotional aspects of conflicts and fostering emotional intelligence, you can create a more harmonious and productive work environment.

The principles of emotionally intelligent conflict transformation

Get ready to discover the key principles for transforming conflicts in an emotionally intelligent way, so you can handle them with grace and effectiveness.

Emotionally intelligent conflict transformation is rooted in self-awareness and understanding of emotions, both your own and others'. It involves recognizing and regulating your emotions, as well as empathizing with the emotions of others involved in the conflict.

By acknowledging and validating emotions, you can create a safe space for open communication and collaborative problem-solving. Another principle is active listening, where you truly listen to the other person's perspective without judgment or interruption. This allows for a deeper understanding and can help in finding common ground.

Building trust and rapport is also crucial in emotionally intelligent conflict transformation. Trust can be established by being authentic and genuine, as well as by demonstrating empathy and respect.

Lastly, it is important to focus on win-win solutions rather than seeking to win at all costs. By working towards mutually beneficial outcomes, you can foster cooperation and create long-lasting resolutions to conflicts.

Emotionally intelligent conflict transformation requires practice and patience, but by applying these principles, you can navigate conflicts with emotional intelligence and achieve positive outcomes.

The potential of emotional intelligence for sustainable resolution of conflicts

Harnessing the power of EQ can pave the path to peaceful and lasting conflict resolution. When emotional intelligence is utilized effectively, it has the potential to transform conflicts in a sustainable way.

By understanding and managing our own emotions, we can approach conflicts with empathy and insight, allowing us to connect with others on a deeper level. This connection fosters open communication, active listening, and a willingness to find common ground.

Emotional intelligence also enables us to recognize and address the underlying emotions and needs that drive conflicts, leading to more meaningful and long-lasting resolutions. By prioritizing emotional intelligence in conflict resolution, we can create a world where conflicts are not only resolved but also transformed into opportunities for growth and understanding.

Emotional Intelligence Strategies for Conflict Transformation

When it comes to conflict transformation, emotional awareness and empathy play a crucial role. Understanding your own emotions and being able to empathize with others can help de-escalate tension and foster understanding.

Non-violent communication is another key strategy that aligns with emotional intelligence, as it emphasizes the importance of expressing oneself assertively and compassionately.

Lastly, cultivating emotional intelligence in peacebuilding and reconciliation processes is essential for creating lasting solutions and healing wounds. By recognizing and addressing the underlying emotions and needs of all parties involved, emotional intelligence can pave the way for transformative and sustainable conflict resolution.

Emotional awareness and empathy in conflict transformation

Imagine yourself in the middle of a heated argument, where you can truly understand and connect with the emotions of the person you're in conflict with, leading to a transformative resolution.

Emotional awareness and empathy play a crucial role in conflict transformation. When you're able to recognize and acknowledge your own emotions, as well as the emotions of others, it opens up a space for genuine understanding and connection.

This awareness allows you to navigate the conflict with empathy, putting yourself in the other person's shoes and truly grasping their perspective. By doing so, you create an environment where both parties feel heard and validated, fostering a sense of trust and mutual respect.

Through emotional awareness and empathy, conflicts can be transformed into opportunities for growth and understanding, ultimately leading to more harmonious and fulfilling relationships.

Non-violent communication and emotional intelligence

Developing your ability to communicate non-violently and harnessing your emotional intelligence can lead to more effective conflict resolution and stronger relationships.

Non-violent communication is a powerful tool that allows you to express your needs and feelings in a way that promotes understanding and connection, rather than escalating conflict.

By actively listening to others and empathizing with their emotions, you can create a safe space for open and honest communication. This approach helps to build trust and fosters mutual respect, which are essential for resolving conflicts in a healthy and constructive manner.

Additionally, by developing your emotional intelligence, you become more aware of your own emotions and better able to regulate them in challenging situations. This self-awareness and self-control enable you to respond to conflicts with empathy and understanding, rather than reacting impulsively or aggressively.

By cultivating these skills, you can transform conflicts into opportunities for growth and deepen your relationships with others.

Cultivating emotional intelligence in peacebuilding and reconciliation processes

Cultivating emotional awareness and understanding can greatly enhance the effectiveness of peacebuilding and reconciliation processes. When individuals involved in these processes develop a deep understanding of their own emotions and those of others, they gain valuable insights into the underlying causes of conflict and can effectively address them.

Emotional intelligence allows individuals to empathize with the experiences and perspectives of others, fostering a sense of connection and trust. By actively listening and validating emotions, peacebuilders can create a safe space for dialogue, encouraging open and honest communication.

This emotional intelligence also enables them to identify and address deep-seated emotional wounds that may be fueling the conflict, allowing for true healing and reconciliation to take place. Moreover, by recognizing and managing their own emotions, peacebuilders can maintain their composure and respond calmly and empathetically to challenging situations.

Ultimately, cultivating emotional intelligence in peacebuilding and reconciliation processes not only helps build lasting peace but also fosters more inclusive and empathetic societies.

XXII. Emotional Intelligence and Social Change

In discussing the subtopic of Emotional Intelligence and Social Change, you'll explore the connection between emotional intelligence and social movements. You'll delve into how emotional intelligence plays a crucial role in building bridges and fostering dialogue among individuals with differing perspectives.

Additionally, you'll examine how emotional intelligence contributes to sustainable social transformation by enabling individuals to navigate conflicts and create positive change.

Emotional Intelligence and Social Movements

When it comes to social change, understanding the role of emotional intelligence is crucial.

This means recognizing how emotions impact our ability to connect with others, build relationships, and mobilize for action.

Whether you're an activist or simply someone passionate about creating positive change, developing emotional intelligence skills will help you navigate the complexities of social advocacy more effectively.

Understanding the role of emotional intelligence in social change

Imagine yourself as a bridge, connecting the power of emotional intelligence to the transformative potential of social change. As you stand in the middle, you see how emotional intelligence acts as a catalyst for social movements, fueling empathy, understanding, and connection among individuals.

It is through emotional intelligence that we're able to truly see and understand the emotions and experiences of others, allowing us to build bridges of solidarity and compassion. Emotional intelligence helps us recognize and navigate our own emotions, enabling us to respond to social issues with empathy and insight.

By incorporating emotional intelligence into social change efforts, we can create a more inclusive and equitable world, where individuals are empowered to address systemic injustices and work towards meaningful change. This understanding of emotional intelligence's role in social change emphasizes the importance of fostering emotional skills and awareness in ourselves and others, as it's through this lens that we can truly build a more empathetic and just society.

Emotional intelligence and activism

As you stand in the middle of the bridge, you can harness the power of your emotional understanding to ignite a fire of activism.

Activism is fueled by passion and a deep sense of empathy, and emotional intelligence plays a crucial role in driving these qualities.

By being in tune with your own emotions and understanding the emotions of others, you can effectively connect with people and inspire change.

Activism often requires engaging in difficult conversations, challenging societal norms, and confronting systemic injustices.

Emotional intelligence allows you to navigate these complexities with empathy and understanding, bridging gaps between different perspectives and fostering a sense of unity.

It enables you to recognize and address the root causes of social issues, empowering you to advocate for justice and equality.

By embracing emotional intelligence, you can amplify your impact as an activist, creating meaningful change in the world.

Emotional intelligence skills for effective social advocacy

Now that you understand the importance of emotional intelligence in activism, let's explore the specific skills that can make your social advocacy efforts more effective.

Building emotional intelligence skills can help you navigate difficult conversations, understand the perspectives of others, and effectively communicate your ideas.

By developing empathy, you can connect with people on a deeper level and inspire them to join your cause.

Active listening is another crucial skill that allows you to truly hear and understand the concerns and experiences of others, helping you to address their needs and create meaningful change.

Additionally, self-awareness and self-regulation can help you manage your emotions in high-pressure situations, ensuring that your advocacy efforts remain focused and productive.

By honing these emotional intelligence skills, you can become a more influential and impactful advocate for social change.

Emotional Intelligence in Building Bridges and Fostering Dialogue

In order to promote understanding and empathy across diverse groups, it's crucial to utilize emotional intelligence. By being attuned to the emotions and perspectives of others, you can bridge gaps and foster meaningful dialogue.

Emotional intelligence is also essential in community organizing and grassroots movements. It allows for effective communication and collaboration.

Lastly, when addressing social issues, emotional intelligence enables individuals to approach problem-solving in a collaborative and empathetic manner. This leads to more sustainable and inclusive solutions.

Emotional intelligence in promoting understanding and empathy across diverse groups

Emotional intelligence plays a crucial role in fostering understanding and empathy among diverse groups. By being aware of and managing one's own emotions, individuals can better navigate interactions with people from different backgrounds and cultures. This self-awareness allows for a deeper understanding of one's own biases and prejudices, enabling us to approach conversations and interactions with an open mind and a willingness to learn.

Additionally, emotional intelligence helps us to recognize and understand the emotions of others, allowing us to respond in a sensitive and empathetic manner. This ability to empathize with others' experiences and perspectives is essential for building bridges across diverse groups and promoting mutual understanding. It enables us to see beyond surface-level differences and connect on a deeper, more human level.

By cultivating emotional intelligence, we can break down barriers, foster dialogue, and create spaces where all individuals feel heard and valued.

Emotional intelligence in community organizing and grassroots movements

You can harness your understanding of others' feelings and effectively connect with like-minded individuals in grassroots movements through your emotional intelligence.

By being attuned to the emotions and needs of those around you, you can build strong relationships and create a sense of unity within your community.

Emotional intelligence allows you to navigate conflicts and disagreements with empathy and understanding, fostering a supportive and inclusive environment.

It helps you recognize the shared values and goals that unite people, allowing you to rally them towards a common cause.

With your emotional intelligence, you can inspire and motivate others, building a strong network of individuals who are passionate about creating positive change.

Your ability to connect on an emotional level will not only strengthen the bond between members of grassroots movements but also enhance their effectiveness in achieving their goals.

Through your emotional intelligence, you can create a space where everyone feels heard, valued, and empowered, making grassroots movements a powerful force for social transformation.

Emotional intelligence in fostering collaborative solutions to social issues

Now that we've explored the role of emotional intelligence in community organizing and grassroots movements, let's delve into how it can be applied to foster collaborative solutions to social issues.

When it comes to addressing complex problems, it's crucial to acknowledge and understand the emotions of all stakeholders involved. By cultivating emotional intelligence, you can establish rapport, build trust, and create a safe space for open dialogue.

This allows for the development of collaborative solutions that take into account the diverse perspectives and experiences of those affected by the social issues at hand. With emotional intelligence as your guide, you can navigate the complexities of these challenges with empathy, insight, and an unwavering commitment to finding common ground and creating positive change.

Emotional Intelligence and Sustainable Social Transformation

In order to create long-term social impact, it's crucial to cultivate emotional intelligence. By understanding and managing your emotions, you can effectively navigate through challenges and build meaningful relationships with others.

Additionally, sustaining emotional well-being and resilience is essential in social change efforts. It allows you to maintain your motivation and cope with the inevitable setbacks along the way.

Finally, ethical leadership combined with emotional intelligence is a powerful combination in driving social transformation. It enables you to inspire and guide others towards positive change while staying true to your values.

Cultivating emotional intelligence for long-term social impact

Developing emotional intelligence can have a lasting impact on society, as studies have shown that individuals with higher emotional intelligence tend to have more successful and fulfilling relationships. By cultivating emotional intelligence, you can not only improve your own personal interactions but also contribute to the overall well-being of society.

Emotional intelligence allows you to understand and manage your own emotions effectively, which in turn enables you to empathize with others and build stronger connections. When you're able to recognize and regulate your emotions, you're better equipped to communicate and resolve conflicts in a respectful and understanding manner. This leads to healthier relationships, both in personal and professional settings, promoting cooperation, collaboration, and ultimately fostering a more harmonious society.

Moreover, emotional intelligence also plays a crucial role in promoting social awareness and empathy towards others. It allows you to understand the emotions and perspectives of different individuals, promoting inclusivity and diversity. By developing emotional intelligence, you can contribute to creating a society that values and respects the emotions and experiences of all its members, leading to long-term social impact and sustainable transformation.

Sustaining emotional well-being and resilience in social change efforts

Maintaining emotional well-being and resilience is crucial for sustaining social change efforts. It allows you to overcome challenges and continue making a positive impact in the world.

In the face of adversity and setbacks, it's essential to prioritize self-care and emotional health. Recognize the importance of taking breaks, seeking support from loved ones, and engaging in activities that bring you joy and rejuvenation.

Embrace the power of self-reflection and introspection to gain insight into your emotions and thoughts. By acknowledging and addressing your own emotional needs, you can cultivate the strength and resilience needed to navigate the complexities of social change.

Remember, you can't pour from an empty cup, so prioritize your well-being to be able to sustain your efforts for the long term.

Ethical leadership and emotional intelligence in social transformation

Leading with integrity and empathy, ethical leaders in social transformation possess a deep understanding of human emotions, allowing them to navigate complex challenges with wisdom and grace.

They recognize that emotions play a crucial role in shaping individual and collective experiences, and they harness this awareness to create inclusive and supportive environments.

By cultivating emotional intelligence, ethical leaders are able to empathize with the diverse perspectives and needs of those they serve, fostering trust and collaboration.

They understand the power dynamics at play in social change efforts and actively work to dismantle oppressive structures, ensuring that marginalized voices are heard and empowered.

Through their genuine care and concern for others, ethical leaders inspire and motivate individuals to join their cause, creating a ripple effect of positive change.

They model emotional resilience, demonstrating that vulnerability and authenticity are not signs of weakness but rather sources of strength.

By leading with integrity and emotional intelligence, ethical leaders in social transformation contribute to a more equitable and compassionate world.

XXIII. Emotional Intelligence in Relationship Building

When it comes to emotional intelligence and interpersonal relationships, building strong emotional connections is essential.

Understanding and managing your emotions, as well as being empathetic towards others, can greatly enhance your relationships.

Additionally, emotional intelligence plays a crucial role in family dynamics, as it allows for effective communication, conflict resolution, and the nurturing of healthy relationships within the family unit.

Emotional Intelligence and Interpersonal Relationships

If you want to build and maintain healthy relationships, emotional intelligence is key.

Understanding your own emotions and being able to empathize with others allows for effective communication and problem-solving, fostering a sense of connection and trust.

Developing emotional intelligence skills such as self-awareness, emotional regulation, and empathy can lead to more fulfilling and satisfying relationships.

Research has shown that individuals with higher emotional intelligence tend to have higher levels of relationship satisfaction, as they're better equipped to navigate conflicts and understand their partner's needs and emotions.

The significance of emotional intelligence in building and maintaining relationships

Understanding and nurturing emotional intelligence is crucial in forming and sustaining meaningful connections with others. When you possess emotional intelligence, you're able to recognize and understand your own emotions, as well as the emotions of those around you.

This awareness allows you to empathize with others, respond appropriately to their needs, and effectively communicate with them. Building and maintaining relationships requires a deep level of emotional connection and understanding.

By cultivating emotional intelligence, you can navigate the complexities of interpersonal interactions and develop stronger bonds with others. You become attuned to the needs and emotions of your loved ones and can provide them with the support and empathy they require.

Additionally, emotional intelligence helps to resolve conflicts and address misunderstandings in a constructive and compassionate manner. It allows you to approach difficult conversations with sensitivity and understanding, which ultimately strengthens your relationships.

In essence, emotional intelligence serves as the foundation for healthy and fulfilling connections with others.

Emotional intelligence skills for effective and fulfilling relationships

Developing strong emotional intelligence skills is like laying a sturdy foundation for a house, providing the necessary support and stability for effective and fulfilling relationships. By honing your emotional intelligence, you gain the ability to understand and manage your own emotions, as well as empathize with and relate to others on a deeper level.

This allows you to navigate conflicts with grace and compassion, communicate effectively, and build trust and intimacy. With emotional intelligence, you become more attuned to the needs and emotions of your partner, fostering a stronger connection and a greater sense of mutual understanding.

Additionally, emotional intelligence helps you recognize and regulate your own emotions, preventing them from negatively impacting your relationships. It allows you to better express yourself, listen actively, and respond empathetically, enhancing the quality of your communication and promoting healthier interactions.

Ultimately, by cultivating emotional intelligence skills, you are equipping yourself with the tools necessary to create and sustain meaningful, satisfying, and lasting relationships.

The impact of emotional intelligence on relationship satisfaction

Enhancing your emotional awareness and ability to effectively manage and connect with others can significantly contribute to the overall satisfaction experienced within your relationships.

Being able to understand and regulate your own emotions allows you to navigate conflicts and challenges in a more constructive manner, fostering a deeper sense of understanding and empathy with your partner.

Additionally, having high emotional intelligence enables you to accurately perceive and respond to your partner's emotions, creating a stronger emotional bond and a greater sense of support and validation.

By developing these skills, you can cultivate a more fulfilling and harmonious relationship, where both you and your partner feel heard, understood, and valued.

Building Strong Emotional Connections

When it comes to romantic relationships, emotional intelligence plays a crucial role in building strong connections.

Understanding and managing your own emotions, as well as being able to empathize with your partner's feelings, are essential skills for fostering emotional intimacy and trust.

Additionally, emotional intelligence helps establish healthy boundaries, allowing for open communication and mutual respect in relationships.

Emotional intelligence in romantic relationships

In romantic relationships, understanding and managing emotions can either strengthen or strain the bond between partners. Emotional intelligence plays a crucial role in fostering a healthy and fulfilling connection.

When both partners possess a high level of emotional intelligence, they're able to effectively communicate their feelings, needs, and desires, leading to a deeper understanding and empathy for one another. This allows for a safe and supportive environment where both individuals feel heard and validated.

Additionally, emotional intelligence enables couples to navigate conflicts and disagreements in a constructive manner, avoiding destructive behaviors such as blame, criticism, or defensiveness. By recognizing and regulating their own emotions, as well as being attuned to their partner's emotional state, couples can cultivate a strong emotional connection that promotes intimacy, trust, and long-term satisfaction.

On the other hand, a lack of emotional intelligence can strain romantic relationships. When individuals struggle to identify and express their emotions, it can lead to misunderstandings, frustration, and a breakdown in communication. This can create a cycle of unresolved conflicts and feelings of disconnection, ultimately eroding the bond between partners.

Therefore, cultivating emotional intelligence within a romantic relationship is essential for fostering a deep and meaningful connection.

Building emotional intimacy and trust

To build emotional intimacy and trust, you need to prioritize open and honest communication with your partner. This means being willing to share your thoughts, feelings, and vulnerabilities, as well as actively listening to your partner without judgment.

By creating a safe space for both of you to express yourselves authentically, you can deepen your connection and understanding of each other. It's important to remember that building emotional intimacy and trust takes time and effort.

It requires both partners to be vulnerable and willing to work through any challenges that arise. By being open and honest with each other, you can create a foundation of trust that will support your relationship in the long run.

Emotional intelligence and healthy boundaries in relationships

Developing emotional intelligence and setting healthy boundaries in relationships is crucial for fostering a strong and balanced connection with your partner. By cultivating emotional intelligence, you gain the ability to understand and manage your own emotions, as well as empathize with your partner's feelings. This allows for open and honest communication, leading to a deeper level of intimacy and trust.

Additionally, establishing healthy boundaries ensures that both you and your partner feel respected and valued within the relationship. It helps create a safe space where each person's needs and limits are acknowledged and honored. By practicing self-awareness and effectively communicating your boundaries, you can create a foundation of trust, respect, and mutual understanding, ultimately leading to a healthier and more fulfilling relationship.

Emotional Intelligence in Family Dynamics

In this discussion, we'll explore the importance of emotional intelligence in various aspects of family dynamics.

You'll learn about the significance of emotional intelligence in parent-child relationships, as it plays a crucial role in fostering a strong bond and understanding between parents and their children.

We'll also discuss the importance of nurturing emotional intelligence in sibling relationships. It helps siblings develop empathy, communication skills, and conflict resolution abilities.

Additionally, we'll delve into the impact of emotional intelligence in multigenerational family dynamics. We'll explore how emotional intelligence can contribute to maintaining harmony and addressing conflicts within extended family relationships.

Emotional intelligence in parent-child relationships

Discover the profound impact of emotional intelligence on your parent-child relationship and unlock the key to nurturing a deeper connection.

When it comes to parenting, emotional intelligence plays a crucial role in fostering a healthy and supportive bond with your child. By cultivating your own emotional awareness and understanding, you can better navigate the ups and downs of parenting, and create a safe and nurturing environment for your child to express their emotions.

As a parent, being emotionally intelligent means being able to recognize and regulate your own emotions, as well as empathize with and validate your child's feelings. It involves actively listening to your child, providing them with space to express themselves, and responding in a compassionate and understanding manner.

By doing so, you can strengthen the parent-child relationship, promote emotional resilience in your child, and lay the foundation for a lifetime of open and honest communication.

So, take the time to develop your emotional intelligence and watch as your parent-child relationship flourishes.

Nurturing emotional intelligence in sibling relationships

Now that we've explored the importance of emotional intelligence in parent-child relationships, let's shift our focus to nurturing emotional intelligence in sibling relationships.

Siblings play a crucial role in shaping our emotional development, as they're often our first companions, confidants, and challengers.

From a young age, siblings have the opportunity to learn and practice important emotional skills such as empathy, communication, and conflict resolution.

As a sibling, you have the power to create a nurturing environment where emotional intelligence can thrive.

By actively listening to your siblings, validating their emotions, and offering support during challenging times, you can foster a strong emotional bond that will benefit both of you throughout your lives.

Remember, emotional intelligence isn't only about understanding and managing your own emotions, but also about recognizing and empathizing with the emotions of others.

By cultivating emotional intelligence in your sibling relationships, you're not only enhancing your own emotional well-being but also creating a foundation for healthy and meaningful connections with others.

Emotional intelligence in multigenerational family dynamics

Get ready to dive into the fascinating world of emotional dynamics in multigenerational families, where the apple doesn't fall far from the tree and generations intertwine like branches on a family tree.

In these intricate webs of relationships, emotional intelligence plays a crucial role. It's the ability to understand and manage emotions, both in oneself and in others.

In multigenerational families, emotional intelligence is not only important for individuals but also for the collective well-being of the family unit. As different generations come together, each with their unique experiences, perspectives, and emotional baggage, conflicts and misunderstandings can arise.

However, emotional intelligence can serve as a bridge, connecting family members and fostering understanding and empathy. It allows individuals to navigate the complexities of family dynamics, recognize and regulate their own emotions, and respond appropriately to the emotions of others.

By developing emotional intelligence in the context of multigenerational family dynamics, we can create a more harmonious and supportive environment for everyone involved.

Addressing conflict and building harmony through emotional intelligence

Take a moment to explore how you can navigate conflict and foster harmony in your multigenerational family by tapping into the power of understanding and managing emotions effectively.

Conflict is inevitable in any family dynamic, especially when different generations come together with their unique perspectives and experiences. However, by developing emotional intelligence, you can address these conflicts in a way that builds understanding and promotes harmony.

Start by recognizing and acknowledging your own emotions and the emotions of others involved in the conflict. This awareness allows you to approach the situation with empathy and understanding, creating a safe space for open communication.

Actively listen to each family member's point of view, validating their emotions and experiences, even if you may not agree with them. By doing so, you demonstrate respect and create an environment where everyone feels heard and valued.

Additionally, try to separate the person from the problem and focus on finding common ground. Encourage open dialogue and problem-solving, allowing each family member to contribute their thoughts and ideas.

Remember, conflict can be an opportunity for growth and understanding if approached with emotional intelligence. By fostering emotional awareness and empathy within your multigenerational family, you can build stronger relationships and create a harmonious environment where everyone feels supported and understood.

XXIV. Emotional Intelligence in Personal and Professional Relationships

When it comes to networking, emotional intelligence plays a crucial role in building and maintaining relationships. Understanding and managing your own emotions, as well as being attuned to the emotions of others, can greatly enhance your ability to connect with and influence people in a professional setting.

In friendships, emotional intelligence allows you to navigate conflicts and communicate effectively, fostering deeper and more meaningful connections.

Lastly, emotional intelligence helps establish and maintain healthy boundaries, allowing you to prioritize your own well-being while still being empathetic and considerate towards others.

Emotional Intelligence and Networking

When it comes to building professional relationships, emotional intelligence plays a crucial role. Understanding and managing your own emotions, as well as being able to empathize with others, can greatly enhance your ability to connect with colleagues and clients.

Networking strategies that incorporate emotional intelligence involve actively listening, showing genuine interest, and adapting your communication style to meet the needs of others.

By leveraging emotional intelligence in your career, you can navigate workplace dynamics more effectively, build stronger relationships, and ultimately advance your professional growth.

Emotional intelligence in building professional relationships

Developing emotional intelligence can greatly enhance your ability to build strong and meaningful professional relationships, but have you ever wondered how it can specifically impact your career success?

When you possess high emotional intelligence, you have the ability to understand and manage your emotions effectively, as well as empathize with others. This enables you to navigate through various social situations with ease, leading to better communication, collaboration, and conflict resolution.

By being aware of your own emotions and those of others, you can respond appropriately, build trust, and foster positive connections. These skills are essential in networking, as they allow you to establish genuine relationships and create a supportive professional network.

Additionally, emotional intelligence enables you to adapt to different working styles, understand and navigate office politics, and effectively influence and motivate others.

Ultimately, by cultivating emotional intelligence, you can create a positive and harmonious work environment that fosters productivity and success.

Networking strategies with emotional intelligence

To effectively network with emotional intelligence, you must actively listen and show genuine interest in others. This allows you to build authentic connections and create a supportive professional network. By actively listening, you demonstrate empathy and understanding, making others feel valued and heard.

This helps you establish trust and rapport, which are crucial for building strong relationships. Additionally, showing genuine interest in others allows you to uncover shared interests and common goals, leading to meaningful conversations and collaborations.

By practicing emotional intelligence in your networking efforts, you can create a supportive network that not only helps you professionally but also provides a sense of belonging and support.

Leveraging emotional intelligence for career advancement

By harnessing the power of emotional insight, you can propel your career forward with greater ease and success.

Emotional intelligence plays a crucial role in career advancement as it allows you to navigate interpersonal relationships, understand your own strengths and weaknesses, and effectively communicate your ideas.

When you have a high level of emotional intelligence, you can build strong and meaningful connections with colleagues, superiors, and clients, which can open doors to new opportunities and collaborations.

Additionally, emotional intelligence helps you to understand and manage your own emotions, enabling you to handle stressful situations, setbacks, and challenges with resilience and grace.

By leveraging your emotional intelligence, you can make informed decisions, adapt to changing circumstances, and demonstrate leadership qualities that are highly valued in the workplace.

Ultimately, by honing your emotional intelligence skills, you can enhance your career prospects and achieve your professional goals with confidence and authenticity.

Emotional Intelligence in Friendships

When it comes to cultivating emotionally intelligent friendships, it's all about being able to understand and manage your own emotions, as well as being able to empathize with and support your friends.

Emotional support and empathy are crucial in friendships because they create a safe space for vulnerability and growth.

Navigating conflicts and maintaining strong friendships with emotional intelligence means being able to communicate openly and honestly, while also considering the emotions and perspectives of both yourself and your friend.

Cultivating emotionally intelligent friendships

Developing emotionally intelligent friendships can be a game-changer in enhancing your overall well-being and happiness. When you cultivate friendships that prioritize emotional intelligence, you create a safe and supportive space where you can openly express your feelings and vulnerabilities. These friendships are built on trust, empathy, and understanding, allowing you to feel truly seen and heard.

You can engage in deep conversations, share your fears and aspirations, and receive valuable feedback without judgment or criticism. Emotionally intelligent friendships also enable you to develop self-awareness and empathy, as you learn to navigate and understand the emotions of others. Through these relationships, you can gain valuable insights into your own emotional patterns and triggers, ultimately leading to personal growth and self-improvement.

By surrounding yourself with emotionally intelligent friends, you create a network of support that uplifts and inspires you, ultimately contributing to your overall happiness and well-being.

Emotional support and empathy in friendships

To truly connect with others on a deeper level, you need to cultivate friendships that provide unwavering emotional support and a genuine understanding of your experiences. Emotional support and empathy are essential components of these friendships, as they create a safe space for you to express your true emotions without fear of judgment or rejection.

When you have friends who are empathetic, they not only validate your feelings but also offer comfort and encouragement during challenging times. They listen attentively, ask insightful questions, and offer guidance when needed, helping you navigate through life's ups and downs.

Having friends who provide emotional support allows you to feel seen, heard, and understood, fostering a sense of belonging and connection. These friendships serve as a valuable source of strength and comfort, reminding you that you are not alone in your experiences and providing a shoulder to lean on when you need it most.

As you cultivate emotionally intelligent friendships, remember to reciprocate the same level of support and empathy to your friends, creating a mutually beneficial and fulfilling bond.

Navigating conflicts and maintaining strong friendships with emotional intelligence

Navigating conflicts and maintaining strong friendships with emotional intelligence can be challenging, but it's worth the effort to foster understanding and connection.

When conflicts arise in friendships, it's important to approach them with empathy and open-mindedness. Instead of resorting to blame or defensiveness, try to understand the underlying emotions and perspectives of both parties involved.

Communicate openly and honestly, expressing your feelings and listening attentively to your friend's point of view. By practicing active listening and validating each other's emotions, you can create a safe space for open dialogue and resolution.

It's also crucial to be aware of your own emotions and how they may affect your responses. Taking a step back to reflect on your feelings and reactions can help you respond in a more thoughtful manner.

Remember, conflicts are a natural part of any relationship, and by approaching them with emotional intelligence, you can strengthen your bond and cultivate a deeper understanding of one another.

Emotional Intelligence and Healthy Boundaries

When it comes to setting and maintaining boundaries, emotional intelligence plays a crucial role. By understanding and managing your emotions effectively, you can communicate your boundaries in a clear and assertive manner, while also considering the emotions and needs of others.

Developing assertiveness skills through emotional intelligence allows you to express your boundaries confidently without being aggressive or passive, fostering healthier and more respectful relationships.

Whether it's in personal or professional relationships, emotional intelligence can help navigate the negotiation of boundaries, ensuring that both parties feel heard, respected, and valued.

Setting and maintaining boundaries with emotional intelligence

Mastering the art of setting and maintaining boundaries will empower you to navigate relationships with emotional intelligence and experience more authentic connections.

When you establish clear boundaries, you communicate your needs and expectations effectively, allowing others to understand and respect your limits. By doing so, you create a safe space for yourself and others, fostering trust and mutual understanding.

Setting boundaries also helps you prioritize self-care and prevent burnout, as you learn to say no when necessary and allocate your time and energy wisely. Additionally, maintaining boundaries requires ongoing self-awareness and assertiveness, which are essential components of emotional intelligence.

It allows you to recognize when your boundaries are being violated and take appropriate action to protect yourself without compromising your relationships. Remember, setting and maintaining boundaries is not about being selfish or controlling; rather, it is about advocating for your own well-being while fostering healthy and respectful connections with others.

Developing assertiveness skills through emotional intelligence

Developing assertiveness skills through emotional intelligence can empower you to confidently communicate your needs and boundaries in relationships, fostering mutual respect and understanding.

By cultivating emotional intelligence, you can become more self-aware of your own emotions and triggers, allowing you to express yourself assertively without resorting to aggression or passivity.

Assertiveness involves expressing your thoughts and feelings in a respectful and direct manner, while also being receptive to the thoughts and feelings of others. This skill can help you establish healthy boundaries, assert your needs, and negotiate conflicts effectively.

It allows you to express yourself authentically and encourages open and honest communication, which can lead to stronger and more fulfilling relationships.

Furthermore, assertiveness allows you to take control of your own life and make decisions that align with your values and goals.

By developing assertiveness skills through emotional intelligence, you can navigate relationships with confidence, assert your needs, and build deeper connections with others.

Emotional intelligence in boundary negotiation in personal and professional relationships

Enhancing your understanding of others' needs and effectively communicating your own can strengthen personal and professional relationships, ultimately fostering a deeper sense of connection and mutual respect.

Emotional intelligence plays a crucial role in boundary negotiation within these relationships. By being aware of your own emotions and recognizing those of others, you can navigate boundaries with empathy and compassion.

This involves understanding the importance of setting healthy boundaries for yourself and respecting the boundaries of others. It requires active listening, empathy, and open communication to ensure that both parties feel heard and understood.

Emotional intelligence allows you to approach boundary negotiation with a mindset of collaboration rather than conflict, seeking solutions that benefit both parties. By cultivating emotional intelligence, you can create a safe and respectful space for boundary negotiation in personal and professional relationships, leading to healthier and more fulfilling connections.

XXV. Conclusion: Embracing Emotional Intelligence in a Changing World

As you conclude your exploration of emotional intelligence in this changing world, it's important to recognize that emotional intelligence is not a destination but rather a lifelong journey.

It's a skill that can always be deepened and refined as you navigate the complexities of personal and professional relationships.

In this ever-evolving world, cultivating emotional intelligence becomes even more crucial as it allows you to adapt, connect, and thrive amidst the challenges and uncertainties that come your way.

The Lifelong Journey of Emotional Intelligence

As you embark on the lifelong journey of emotional intelligence, you'll discover the importance of continual growth and development. It's through ongoing practice and self-reflection that you'll deepen your understanding and mastery of this essential skill.

Emotional intelligence isn't a one-time accomplishment, but rather a lifelong pursuit. It'll serve as a foundation for your success and well-being.

Continual growth and development of emotional intelligence

To truly level up your emotional intelligence, you've got to keep on hustlin' and put in the work to continuously expand your understanding and development.

Emotional intelligence is not a fixed trait; it's a lifelong journey of growth and self-awareness. It requires the willingness to reflect on your emotions, understand their origins, and explore how they impact your thoughts and actions.

This continual growth and development of emotional intelligence is a process that requires patience, self-compassion, and a commitment to self-improvement. It's about being open to feedback, seeking out opportunities for learning, and embracing discomfort as a catalyst for personal growth.

By actively engaging in this process, you can develop a deeper understanding of yourself and others, cultivate empathy and compassion, and enhance your ability to navigate and regulate your emotions.

Remember, emotional intelligence is not a destination, but rather a lifelong journey that requires dedication and effort. So keep hustlin' and never stop striving to expand your emotional intelligence.

The importance of ongoing practice and self-reflection

Engaging in ongoing practice and self-reflection allows you to deepen your understanding of yourself and others, fostering empathy and compassion while enhancing your ability to navigate and regulate your emotions.

By consistently practicing emotional intelligence skills, such as active listening and self-awareness, you develop a greater sense of self-awareness, enabling you to identify and manage your own emotions more effectively. This self-reflection also helps you to recognize patterns and triggers in your emotional responses, allowing you to make conscious choices about how you want to react in different situations.

Furthermore, ongoing practice and self-reflection enable you to develop a deeper understanding of others' emotions, enhancing your ability to empathize with their experiences and perspectives. This increased empathy and compassion not only strengthens your relationships but also allows you to navigate conflicts and challenges with greater ease and understanding.

Ultimately, by dedicating yourself to ongoing practice and self-reflection, you can cultivate a high level of emotional intelligence that positively impacts both your personal and professional life.

Emotional intelligence as a lifelong skill for success and well-being

Developing emotional intelligence is like planting a seed that grows into a flourishing garden, enriching all aspects of your life for lasting success and well-being. It's a lifelong skill that requires ongoing practice and self-reflection.

Emotional intelligence allows you to navigate through life's challenges with grace and understanding, fostering stronger relationships and effective communication. By understanding and managing your own emotions, you gain the ability to empathize with others, leading to deeper connections and a greater sense of fulfillment.

As you cultivate emotional intelligence, you become more self-aware, recognizing your own strengths and weaknesses, and in turn, you're able to make more informed decisions. This heightened level of self-awareness also enables you to regulate your emotions, allowing you to respond to situations in a calm and rational manner.

Ultimately, emotional intelligence is not only essential for personal growth, but it also plays a significant role in professional success. It enhances leadership skills, promotes effective teamwork, and helps build a positive work environment.

By continuously nurturing and developing your emotional intelligence, you lay the foundation for a life filled with fulfillment, resilience, and overall well-being.

Cultivating Emotional Intelligence in a Changing

World

As you navigate through an evolving society, it's crucial to adapt your emotional intelligence skills to meet the changing needs of those around you.

By embracing diversity and inclusivity through emotional intelligence, you can create a more understanding and compassionate world.

Looking ahead, the future of emotional intelligence holds immense potential to impact society in profound ways. It'll foster healthier relationships, promote empathy, and foster a sense of belonging for all.

Adapting emotional intelligence skills in an evolving society

Adapting our emotional intelligence skills is crucial in a changing society, where our ability to understand and manage our emotions determines our success and well-being.

As the world continues to evolve at a rapid pace, we're faced with new challenges and complexities that require us to navigate a wide range of emotions.

It's no longer enough to simply be aware of our feelings; we must also develop the skills to regulate and express them effectively.

In this ever-changing landscape, being emotionally intelligent allows us to adapt and thrive in the face of uncertainty. It enables us to build strong relationships, make sound decisions, and effectively communicate our needs and boundaries.

By understanding our emotions and the emotions of others, we can cultivate empathy and compassion, fostering a more inclusive and understanding society.

As we navigate the complexities of this evolving world, our emotional intelligence becomes a powerful tool that helps us not only survive but also thrive.

So, let's embrace the opportunity to develop and refine our emotional intelligence skills, knowing that they're essential for our personal and collective growth.

Embracing diversity and inclusivity through emotional intelligence

By embracing diversity and inclusivity, we can foster a society where emotional intelligence skills naturally flourish.

When we open ourselves up to different perspectives and experiences, we create an environment that encourages empathy and understanding.

By valuing and appreciating the unique backgrounds and characteristics of individuals, we not only promote inclusivity, but we also create opportunities for personal growth and development.

Understanding and embracing diversity allows us to challenge our biases and assumptions, and encourages us to broaden our perspectives.

It cultivates a sense of empathy and compassion, as we learn to appreciate the experiences and emotions of others.

In turn, this enhances our emotional intelligence, enabling us to navigate complex social situations with ease and sensitivity.

By embracing diversity and inclusivity, we not only create a more harmonious society, but we also empower ourselves to become more emotionally intelligent individuals.

The future of emotional intelligence and its potential impact on

society

The future holds immense potential for emotional intelligence, transforming society into a more compassionate and understanding place where connections and empathy thrive.

As emotional intelligence continues to gain recognition and importance, its impact on society will become even more profound.

With a greater focus on emotional well-being and understanding, individuals will be equipped with the skills to navigate complex emotions and build healthier relationships.

This will lead to a society that values empathy, inclusivity, and diversity, as people become more attuned to the emotions and experiences of others.

Emotional intelligence has the power to break down barriers, foster collaboration, and promote a sense of belonging, ultimately creating a world where compassion and understanding are at the forefront of our interactions.

By cultivating emotional intelligence, we can shape a future that is more harmonious, accepting, and interconnected.

Don't miss out!

Visit the website below and you can sign up to receive emails whenever Adam Poliman publishes a new book. There's no charge and no obligation.

https://books2read.com/r/B-A-VSRY-KAHNC

BOOKS 2 READ

Connecting independent readers to independent writers.

Did you love *The Emotion Code: Decoding Emotional Intelligence*?
Then you should read *The Art of Social Intelligence: Mastering the Skills
of Effective Communication*[1] by Adam Poliman!

[2]

"The Art of Social Intelligence: Mastering the Skills of Effective Communication" is a comprehensive and transformative guide that empowers individuals to excel in their interpersonal communication abilities and elevate their social intelligence to new heights. In today's interconnected world, effective communication has become a paramount skill for personal and professional success. This book goes beyond superficial techniques and provides a deep understanding of the underlying principles that drive meaningful and impactful communication.

---

1. https://books2read.com/u/4jNnKv

2. https://books2read.com/u/4jNnKv

Through practical techniques, insightful strategies, and real-life examples, this book offers a roadmap for developing and honing essential communication skills. Discover the art of active listening, where you will learn to truly engage with others, understand their perspectives, and respond with empathy and clarity. Explore the nuances of nonverbal communication, mastering the subtle language of body movements, facial expressions, and gestures to convey messages with precision and authenticity.

Delving into the realm of emotional intelligence, this book unravels the power of self-awareness and emotional regulation, enabling you to navigate challenging situations with grace and tact. Learn the art of conflict resolution, acquiring the skills to identify, manage, and resolve conflicts constructively, while preserving relationships and fostering collaboration. Gain a deep understanding of cultural sensitivity and diversity, embracing differences and effectively communicating across cultural boundaries.

Unlock the secrets of persuasion and influence, understanding the psychology behind human decision-making and leveraging it ethically to inspire, motivate, and effect positive change. Sharpen your public speaking and presentation skills, captivating audiences with impactful storytelling, engaging visuals, and confident delivery.

Furthermore, this book addresses the evolving landscape of digital communication, offering guidance on effective virtual communication, navigating the nuances of email and instant messaging etiquette, and managing online interactions and social media presence with finesse and professionalism.

"The Art of Social Intelligence" also highlights the importance of building and nurturing relationships. Discover the power of networking and relationship-building techniques, fostering connections that can open doors to new opportunities and collaborations. Additionally, explore communication in personal relationships, including family, friends, and romantic partners, learning effective techniques to express love, navigate conflicts, and deepen emotional connections.

Throughout this journey of self-discovery and skill development, you will find practical exercises, reflective prompts, and actionable tips that will enhance your learning experience and help you apply the concepts in real-life situations. By mastering the art of social intelligence, you will unlock your full potential in every social interaction, enriching your personal and professional relationships and experiencing a profound positive impact on your life.

Read more at https://optimizationtime.com.

Also by Adam Poliman

The Power of Time: Transform Your Life through Effective Time Management

Unleashing The Power Of Reading

Unlocking the Power of Critical Thinking: Strategies for Effective Problem-Solving

Efficiency Unleashed: Mastering Productivity Tips and Hacks for Success

The Art of Social Intelligence: Mastering the Skills of Effective Communication

Destined For Greatness: Mastering The Art Of Goal Setting

Mind Over Temptation: Building Self-Discipline In A Distracted World

The Emotion Code: Decoding Emotional Intelligence

The Growth Mindset Advantage: Thriving Through Lifelong Learning

Unleashing Your Potential: A Guide To Personal Development And Self-Improvement

Watch for more at https://optimizationtime.com.

About the Author

Adam Poliman is a renowned author in the personal improvement space, dedicated to helping individuals unlock their full potential and lead fulfilling lives. With a passion for personal growth and a deep understanding of human psychology, Adam combines his expertise with practical insights to empower readers to make positive changes. His thought-provoking books offer actionable strategies and transformative techniques that inspire readers to overcome challenges, cultivate resilience, and achieve their goals. Through his writing, Adam seeks to guide readers on a transformative journey of self-discovery, encouraging them to embrace personal development and create a life of purpose and fulfillment.

Read more at https://optimizationtime.com.

www.ingramcontent.com/pod-product-compliance
Lightning Source LLC
Chambersburg PA
CBHW021152160726
47994CB00001B/168